ITALIAN
MODERN

GIOVANNI ALBERA
NICOLAS MONTI

DESIGN BY WILLIAM A. EWING

ITALIAN
MODERN

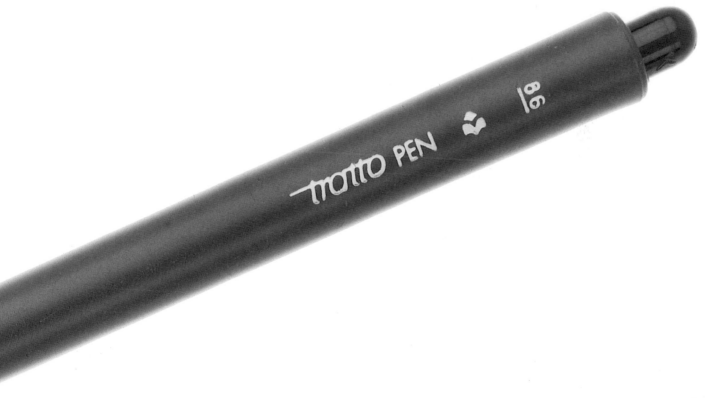

A DESIGN HERITAGE

RIZZOLI
NEW YORK

Acknowledgments

For support and advice, warm thanks to our publisher, Gianfranco Monacelli, and to our editors, David Morton and Robert Janjigian.

We also extend thanks to all the industrial designers, architects and manufacturers who participated and cooperated with us in the initial research for this book, providing the necessary written information and photographs. For his assistance in locating historical material, we especially mention Ferruccio Dilda of the Triennale Library. For helping to input and process the overwhelming amount of information and photographs, we thank Elena Galliani and Rosalba Pasini. We are much indebted to Paola Mola, Ferdinando Monti, Alberica Pellerey, Anna Winand and, above all, to Elena Elli, our research associate, for reading the manuscript, discussing our ideas and offering helpful advice throughout this project.

First published in the United States of America in 1989 by
RIZZOLI INTERNATIONAL PUBLICATIONS, INC.
597 Fifth Avenue, New York, NY 10017

Copyright © Giovanni Albera and Nicolas Monti

Library of Congress
Cataloging-in-Publication Data

Albera, Giovanni.
   Italian modern, a design heritage.
   Bibliography: p.
   Includes index.
   1. Design—Italy—History—20th century.   2. Design, Industrial—Italy.   I. Monti, Nicolas.   II. Title.
NK1452.A1A43 1989   745.2'0945   88-43420
ISBN 0-8478-1034-8

Typeset by David E. Seham Associates Inc., Metuchen, N.J.
Printed and bound by Dai Nippon, Tokyo, Japan

ENDPAPER: Abet Laminati's Pattern 216.

CONTENTS

▼ The Torso armchair was designed in
1983 by Paolo Deganello for Cassina.

Introduction

Italy's position as a center for international design is
unquestionable. But, in the design of the world and in the
world of design, why always the Italians? For automobiles
and furniture, computers and tableware, even Nikon cameras for the Japanese, or Mercedes-Benz automobiles for
the West Germans, Italian designers are *the* creative force.
Luigi Caccia Dominioni answered, ''We are simply the
best, we have more fantasy, more culture, and we man-
age better in the role of mediators between the past and
the future. That is why our design is more beautiful and
up-to-date than that of other countries.''[1]

The Italians seem to have, almost by ancestral right,
that which other nationalities can acquire only at the cost
of an extensive education. Bruno Sacco, responsible for
the design department of Daimler/Benz, gave his thoughts
to an interviewer: ''It's a question of the spontaneity of
the message, for which we are particularly gifted. The his-
torical/cultural heritage that every Latin has received allows
him to refer rapidly to the fruits of his own upbringing.''[2]

Italian design expresses a culture able to connect
itself with tradition, recovering and applying the pre-exist-
ing figurative heritage; a recycling of the past which has
had a long tradition in Italy. Ernesto Nathan Rogers, one of
the fathers of Italian Rationalism, sustained, ''There are no
real modern works that do not have authentic foundations
in the tradition.''[3]

The protagonists of Italian design seem to be
endowed with an extraordinary longevity. An incredible
number of architect/designers trained before World War II
are today still extraordinarily active and able. Impervious to
trends, they foster a design inspired by the functionalist
canons, a direct inheritance from the Bauhaus. Bringing
together pragmatism and technical knowledge to a solidly
classic culture, they were able to make their own mark on
all the production from the post-war period to the present

day, expressing a culture of design full of imagination and individualism, rich in human and poetic values.

But Italian design was also able to keep up with technological progress, with the discoveries of new materials and the inventions of new machines. Italian designers take pride in their close relationship with the world of industry and their capacity to integrate its innovations into their work. The vocational quality of draftsmanship, a deep aesthetic sensitivity, an extraordinary sense of spatial stratification obtained through the care for and the invention of detail, the recognition of the value of materials, the perception of a continuity of environmental image and a lasting tradition of excellent workmanship and technical quality are part of the uncommon Italian heritage and the determining ingredients in the best Italian industrial design.

Design in Italy was born and developed in a relatively limited geographic area. Around the city of Milan, there are concentrated, for a number of geographic, economic and historic circumstances, the greater part of the energies both in design and production relative to the modern applied arts (or to the decorative and industrial arts), to the extent of creating an essential cultural crossroads. This centralization of talent and production was initially relevant to Italy, but little by little came to influence the rest of Europe and the whole world. Milan is the magnetic city, which since the 1930s has attracted the best talent from the rest of Italy,[4] and, since the 1950s, from abroad. Designers from Switzerland, the Netherlands, the United States and Japan (Perry King, Andries Van Onck, Richard Sapper and Isao Hosoe, to cite but a few) have found the city an ideal workplace for its central position in terms of its principal clients, specialized publishing and exhibition facilities, as well as a particularly favorable cultural climate. Italian design and its history are actually so identifiable with this city that one could almost talk about

Milanese rather than *Italian* design.

Milan, at the heart of the most industrialized region of Italy, is also the most important center of finance and enterprise in the country. Its cold, foggy winters, hot, smoggy summers, and a reputation for exuding as much charm as Detroit or Liverpool, probably have something to do with the city's Calvinistic mentality and the general visitor perception of the Milanese as pragmatic, hard-working moneymakers. Milan, besides its traditionally strong industrial muscle, also dominates in the service industry sectors (particularly in communication and advertising), while as the home of the Italian stock exchange and most of the national and international investment banks, the city holds the country's purse strings. Furthermore, Milan is also the most dynamic and lively center for the creation and promotion of Italian cultural products. In terms of prosperity, productivity and creativity, Milan is the nation's de facto capital.

Culturally closer to central Europe, from which it absorbed an organized view of life during the decades of Austrian rule, but also markedly influenced by a typically Mediterranean creative component, the city defies neat labels; its ideas and energies, its power and products all have a dual nature. The city's location, equidistant from and very near both the Alps and the Mediterranean Sea, seems ideal for a meeting point of sophisticated Latin sensuality with rigorous central European industrial culture. As a consequence, design born in Milan is the natural synthesis and expression of two souls; an idolatry of efficiency blended with a warm regard for culture. The objects which result are the expression and the ornament of an evolved and throughly modern life that is, at the same time, rigorously rational and exceptionally refined.

The professional origin and the cultural matrix of the designer can vary extremely, but the Milanese ambience into which design has sunk its roots is dominated by architects. Giò Ponti wrote, "Italians should love architecture because Italy is made half by God and half by architects. God made the plains, hills, waters and skies, but the profiles of the domes, facades, steeples and towers are things created by architects. In Venice, God made only the water and the sky, and, unintentionally, the architects did the rest."[5]

While the professional origin and cultural matrix of a designer can greatly differ, Italy was perhaps the first country where the industrial design and architecture professions were not separated. This is a fact which today is considered to be understood, but that in other countries was, up until a few years ago, more the exception than the rule. Architects recognized at once a very fertile terrain in the problematics of the culture of industrial design projects. They have always realized that industrial design can be an extremely definite fact, with its intention of direct contact with an individual's daily life, enabling a designer to make himself and his ideas come into contact with the public in a much more direct way than through architecture.

Edoardo Persico, in the years of the birth of Italian design, wrote that design could be a way of going "beyond architecture." Lodovico Belgiojoso, one of the founders of the BBPR studio[6] defined design "as one of the fundamental components in the making of architecture, and as a tool for the correct definition of the details inside even a large scale work, both as a means of following and applying the technology and industrialization in the constructive processes, and as a discipline in itself."

Vico Magistretti actually turned upside-down the order of importance in the scale of the possible operations of the architect, saying, "I believe that it is much more useful in order to diffuse a certain tendency, to design a small object for a relatively big series, rather than a single building. Few live in the building, some see it and discuss it, but it remains a proposal outside of the life of those who live in it or those who see it. An object, on the other hand, by the simple virtue of having been chosen by the person who uses it, is much more likely to determine an influence on the user, perhaps indirect and subtle, but even so just as authentic and effective at suggesting a different way of understanding the space-object relationship in the home and in the way of living."[7]

In the beginning, the architect's involvement came about for the most part in the furnishings sector. Until the 1930s, contrary to the artisan custom of transforming every item of furnishings into a sort of domestic monument, the architects sought a global planning of the home environment, including utility objects from the radio to the first household appliances, underlining their functional aspects. Moreover, in the period before World War II, there was an additional political factor. In fact, certain ideas that were impossible to translate into architecture, partly because of the hostility of fascism, partly for the provincialism that dominated Italian society, could be expressed in the field of industrial design.

The economic factor, whose weight has so often been felt, cannot be ignored. Design gives many architects the chance to supplement the scarcity of work in a strictly architectural field. To diversify in hard times may be more a necessity than a choice.

In Italy, from the post-war period to the present day, a particular historical situation and heavy political pressures have not allowed some of the great themes of architecture to be tackled and resolved efficiently. The failure has involved, indifferently, urbanism, territorial planning, housing problems and building industrialization. Only in industrial design was found the freedom and openness

◄ Vittorio Rigettieri's Trottola glassware line, designed in 1986 for Cenedese & Albarelli, consists of champagne glasses, bowls, decanters and vases.

that allowed a design culture to express itself with sufficient completeness and maturity.

At the end of the 1960s, Jonathan De Pas, Donato D'Urbino and Paolo Lomazzi asked themselves: why design in Italy, and not, rather, in swinging London or in the States or in Holland, where the cultural ambience would seem to be more stimulating by far? They answered, ". . . the revered Rogers said in the 1950s, 'The architect designs everything: from the spoon to the city.' So the graduate began to search at once for a city to design. After some years of meetings of political parties, of factions, of boards of education, of town councils, of committees, of intercommunal planning councils, of (when time could be found) studies and of design; after having produced a plan approved by all and applied by none, and having obtained, for services rendered, the job of doing a town hall or a sewage system, and having honorably followed it through; after all that, one began to consider the spoon with a benevolent eye. In England and elsewhere, they built new towns, while we, among many, came to the field of design and, in particular, to the objects for the home. Partly because after much designing (and not realizing) model dwellings and public housing (in fact, unit dwellings), we got a certain idea of living, partly because the object for the home allowed a global proposal, that is, instead of designing the body of someone else's car, we ourselves offered the idea, the form and the norms of use."[8]

Design in Italy was thus stolen from the technicians and passed into the hands of professionals with a training and a cultural broad-mindedness very different from that of the traditional industrial designer. The exceptional involvement of architects in the vicissitudes of Italian design found its natural result in products that, on the one hand, mirrored the drive towards functional innovation, and, on the other hand, conserved a strong image with evident recall of an architectural project.

A second consequence of this involvement is the quite original position of the Italian industrial designer in relation to the client. In fact, almost all professionals work outside the manufacturing structure, even when their respective relationships with the firm extend over a long period of time. Even more unusual was a kind of mixed general consultancy on a part-time basis with a firm, and, up to the 1970s, the uncommon arrangement was an actual design department. The designer is rarely an actual employee of the industries, and keeps a cultural independence (that could sometimes seem excessive, and even detrimental, but that is implicit in his development as a free-lancer) that allows him to keep in sight the social and cultural context in which he operates, and into which he must fit his creations. "To stay out, to be a consultant, meant also to be able to continually draw news and information from public life, and from the surrounding ambience, and thus maintain an intellectual elasticity that the employee, by and by, began to lose, being distracted by the internal problems."[9] A critical commitment, sometimes politicized to an exaggerated degree, distinguishes him from his foreign colleagues.

Contrary to his fellow professionals abroad who tend to specialize in a much more rigid way, the Italian industrial designer prefers, traditionally, to apply himself to the most differing fields of design. As Mario Bellini wrote, "This way of working, unthinkable in any other country, pushed me, in the effort not to lose my identity, to the constant research of a common base, of a connection whose validity would exceed the traditional subdivision of the professions, based more on the corresponding merchandising or academic-disciplinary differences than on a substantial design difference. I believe I have found a kind

▶ The Serenissimo low table, designed by Massimo and Lella Vignelli with David Law, was introduced by Acerbis International in 1985.

of *invariant* dimension, across the different disciplines, in what you could call the *living relationship* between man and his physio-environmental structures (machines, furnishings, objects, architecture); a common relationship thus to all in the *continuum* of the living experience."[10]

The term *Industrial Design* is commonly used to indicate those aspects of design whose aim is to determine the aesthetic qualities of an object that is mass produced with industrialized methods and systems. Mass production means produced in series, that is, every piece is made absolutely identical to the next one and the same as the prototype. The birth of industrial design is thus connected to the rise of mass production techniques.

The *formal qualities* of the object do not refer only to the outside appearance, but are finalized at the obtaining of a coherent unity between the image, the structure and the specific function of a utilitarian object. The design of the object, as a creative operation, has that quality of uniqueness, and of distinction, typical of the work of art, that sets it apart from any other design, and that constitutes its true identity.

Industrial design embraces all aspects of the human environment that are influenced by industrial production. A border discipline between the humanities and the sciences, it has tried to find its own field of action, sometimes marginal, sometimes decisive, in some cases reduced to a mere operation of cosmetics, in others involving the very mechanisms of technological transformation. The designer's common aim is to build a more rational, pleasant and beautiful human society, even with regard to its minor aspects, such as a television or an alarm clock.

Most writing about design matters appears in obscure academic texts, written by and for scholars, and seems to be either monumentally boring or predictably pretentious. The difficulty is innate in tackling subjects more immediately described through images. The history of industrial design is, first of all, a story of objects, and the authors of this book sympathize with the declaration of some of the major industrial designers who refuse to reduce their own work into words. Mario Bellini said, "To make a declaration of your own poetic conception obviously presupposes that you have one, and that it is simple (dare I say banal) enough and crystallized enough, to be able to transmit it better in a written form than by means of actually practicing it, that it should be the verification of that conception, and the fuel in a mutual continuity between thought and design."[11]

The architects De Pas, D'Urbino and Lomazzi commented, "Every now and then they ask us what design means to us, and we reply: our work. Then they ask us what our poetic conception is, and we tell them to look at the things we do, so they complain that we haven't answered."[12] But the most concise of all is Richard Sapper who said, "I think that a designer must explain himself through his work, not through verbal explanations. Thus, I have nothing to say about my work in general."[13]

The intention of this book is to give the reader a chance to acquire a wide view of the horizon in the fast changing scene of the Italian culture of design, to see and share the very best of a world that combines function with beauty, utility with imagination and innovation with social responsibility.

The brief historical reconnaisance that follows is aimed at individualizing and identifying the political-economic context in which Italian design has its roots. The intention is not only to compose a history of masterpieces, that are abundant anyway, but also to show how these are the result of a professional continuity, developed over decades of labor and experimentation. Only by a broad

The History

Before World War II

panorama is it possible to get a complete picture of the aspirations and realizations of Italian design, also considering the difficulty of giving a coherent image of a phenomenon discontinuous in itself.

Notes

[1] Luigi Caccia Dominioni, *In aller Welt,* n.199, 1/1986

[2] *In aller Welt,* no. 199, 1/1986

[3] Ernesto N. Rogers, *Casabella,* n.199, 1954

[4] "In the late 20s I came to Milan the way some people go to Mecca: to pay tribute to an exceptional city." Eugenio Montale, "Vivere a Milano", *Corriere della Sera,* January 27, 1970

[5] Giò Ponti, *Autobiografia lampo,* February 21, 1977

[6] The firm BBPR is named after its principals: Gianni Banfi, Lodo Belgiojoso, Aurel Peressutti, Ernesto Rogers

[7] Vico Magistretti, *Milano 70/70,* Milan: Museo Poldi Pezzoli, vol. 3, p. 168

[8] J. De Pas, D. D'Urbino, P. Lomazzi, "I nostri buoni propositi", *Milano 70/70,* Milan: Museo Poldi Pezzoli, vol. 3, p. 166

[9] A. Martorana, *Storie e progetti di un designer italiano, quattro lezioni di Ettore Sottsass,* Florence: Alisea, April 1983, p. 23

[10] Mario Bellini, *Atlante del Design Italiano,* Milan: Fabbri, 1980, p. 277

[11] Mario Bellini, *Atlante del Design Italiano,* Milan: Fabbri, 1980, p. 277

[12] J. De Pas, D. D'Urbino, P. Lomazzi, *Atlante del Design Italiano,* Milan: Fabbri, 1980, p. 299

[13] Richard Sapper, *Atlante del Design Italiano,* Milan: Fabbri, 1980, p. 289.

In Italy, the development of industrial design started later than in other central European countries or the United States. The absence of a tradition in this field was largely due to the country's late industrialization, which, except in a few specific branches such as aeronautics and the automobile industry, did not really begin until the 1930s. Until then, Italian industrialization could not stand comparison with the levels already reached in central Europe.

On November 4, 1918, Italy signed the armistice with the Austro-Hungarian Empire. A few days later the word PEACE appeared in letters a foot high on the front pages of the world press. The *greatest war in history* was over at last. Amid the fluttering flags, the victorious clangor of the brass bands and the fresh memories of disaster and mourning, many fostered the hope that it was possible to take up again the threads of the variegated loom pattern which had been interrupted at the outbreak of World War I.

The prevailing cultural climate was still that of the 19th century: late art nouveau taste and customs, common throughout Europe, still dominated; opera music and the waltz had nothing yet to fear from the charleston and the fox-trot. The façades of villas and townhouses still denoted 19th century eclecticism, and the drawing rooms of the Italian bourgeoisie were preferably fitted with heavily-carved imitation Renaissance furniture, and illuminated by the decadent light of *belle époque* lampshades. Tito Lessi's realistic illustrations of the *Decamerone* continued to shock, and the summit of sinfulness was still the vague eroticism in the novels by Guido da Verona. The magnificent, slightly Russian-style stage settings by the Benois dynasty of scenographers for the operas at La Scala continued to raise enthusiasm. The Italian and foreign cultural vanguards were ignored; the futurist storm was still recent and had left some traces, but apparently without a very deep effect. Giorgio De Chirico probably expressed the opinion of the majority when in 1919 he wrote in the magazine *Valori Plastici,* "Personally I think that Italy needed futurism as much as it needed the war; it came just like the war came, because it was bound to come, but we could very well have done without it." Everything seemed to link up again with the situation as it had been at the moment of going to the front.

It was, of course, an illusion; the pre-war world belonged to the past. For Italy, the war lasted only three years, but it was not just an interlude, it was a clean cut in its history. The curtain had definitely fallen on the 19th century.

Contrary to the illusion cherished by cultural life, the world of economy and industry realized that time had not stood still and that the war had provided new opportunities for growth and renewal. In fact, the war had spurred the development of industrial plants not only in number, but in terms of the rationalization and standardization of production, with a rapid technical evolution, particularly in the fields considered of strategic importance, such as transportation and communications. Yet, in most sectors of industry, especially those not essential to warfare, the manufacturing processes, even those with large output, were still mainly based on handcraft.

Immediately after the end of the Great War, the young Italian democracy went through a period of social unrest, culminating in the occupation of factories in 1920. Against the demonstrations and strikes, the old liberal members of Parliament themselves invoked a *strong state,* and with the hope that authority would be reestablished, they tolerated fascist violence.

The serious problems connected with the conversion of war industries and the economic crises of 1926 and 1929 were not enough to stop unprecedented industrial development. From 1923 onward—parallel to the rise and consolidation of fascism, which installed a policy of tax abatement, high import duties and restriction of trade union power—Italy's production and new fields of development took an impressive flight. This new takeoff concerned mainly industry and commerce, and less the small artisan enterprises. The time was ripe to give more scope to the decorative arts, which had not yet been freed from a great but weary tradition, but were soon to become an integral factor in the industrial manufacturing processes.

The early 1920s were marked by the cultural exploits of Gabriele D'Annunzio, posthumous art nouveau expressions, unaccepted futuristic claims (Filippo Tommaso Marinetti and his followers continued to collect tomatoes on all the country's stages) and folkloric reminiscences. With a few outstanding exceptions, the cultural world seemed ill-prepared for renewal, and the general mood was drowsy.

The situation was contrasted with the turbulent vitality of an emerging society. In the period between the two World Wars, there was a progressive concentration of the most important initiatives in only two cities, Milan and Turin, with an extension on the administrative level in Rome. The revival of Italy's economy was based mainly on the dynamism of the industries in Lombardy and its capital, Milan. Here, the most important publishing houses, such as Treves, Bestetti and Ricordi, established their headquarters. Here, the Milan Trade Fairs had started to give a new impulse to the various branches of industry, such as textile manufacturers in the Como area, or furniture producers in the Brianza region.

Although polytechnicians and industrial managers would still remain influenced by the deep-rooted conviction that art and technique were incompatible, there were already some schools where these subjects were taught in

▶ The 2633 table was designed by Pietro Chiesa, Jr. for Fontana Arte in 1932.

parallel programs. The Umanitaria school of Milan, founded in 1922, and the I.S.I.A. (High School for Industrial Arts) in Monza turned out qualified designers. Teaching was based on direct experimentation with the traditional handicraft methods that prevailed in workshops, as well as critical experimentation with the most recent techniques.

By the end of the 1920s, Milan had become the central battleground for modern architecture. Architecture, handicrafts and the decorative arts followed a tendency that corresponded with the *Novecento* movement in contemporary painting and sculpture. The taste for neoclassicism that typified the work of the *Novecento* followers characterized the furniture and decorative elements designed by young architects such as Emilio Lancia, Giovanni Muzio, Giuseppe De Finetti and Michele Marelli. The same taste pervaded the design of crystal objects by Balsamo Stella, glass products by Pietro Chiesa, Jr., furniture by Guglielmo Ulrich and ceramics by Giò Ponti and Guido Andloviz. In its approach to the decorative arts, the *Novecento* was, on the whole, moderately avant-garde and had many stylistic elements in common with Rationalism, although the latter current saw order and reason more as a strict relationship between function and use, whereas the Novecentist gave great value to classicism and tradition.

The exponents of both movements had intricate relations with the regime. When some years after having come to power, the fascists started paying attention to architecture and the decorative arts, they did so with the same eclecticism and opportunistic intuition that were typical of Mussolini's political and cultural policies. Italy was going through a strange period. Everyone seemed to perceive in the fascist movement the opportunity to carry out his own ideas. Intellectuals of opposed tendencies thought they could influence fascism, to push it one day in the *right* direction. Many expressed openly their belief in the

fascist revolution. Until the end of the 1930s, the Academy, the Neoclassicists of the *Novecento* movement and the Rationalists fought for supremacy in the fascist ideology. The different design philosophies coexisted thanks to the regime's great capacity for digesting them all.

As a consequence, within the regime, the artistic movements formed a center, a left and a right wing. The younger generation especially demanded from the fascist regime a place for new artistic expressions on an international scale. Despite the manifold pressures, fascism's cultural policy did not give any precise answers for these problems. The regime's basic neutrality did not withhold it from recognizing and sometimes exploiting the value of mass communication of the arts and crafts.

The Italian movement of *Rational* architecture, adhering to the so-called modern movement, started in Milan in the autumn of 1926 with the foundation of the *Gruppo 7*. The group's program stated, "The new architecture must be the result of strict adherence to logic, to rationality. The rules must be dictated by rigid constructivism. Speaking of construction in series seems to many a diminution of the concept of art. Variety does not necessarily mean beauty. Simplicity does not mean poverty."[1]

Only in 1930, with the foundation of the MIAR (*Movimento italiano per l'architettura razionale*), was this tendency publicly codified. The following year, the appearance of Bauhaus-inspired furniture by Luigi Figini and Gino Pollini, but, above all, the design of the Notari Bookstore in Milan by Luciano Baldessari, which recalled German expressionism, caused a scandal, but also immediate imitations. The new design philosophy would assert itself with the epoch-making interior decoration and furnishings of Baldessari's Bar Craja, also in Milan. Raffaello Giolli dedicated his magazine *Problemi d'arte attuale* (Oct. 1927) "to those who ignore that, beside paintings, alarm clocks and

▶ Gió Ponti's 0024 ceiling light fixture was designed in 1931 for Fontana Arte.

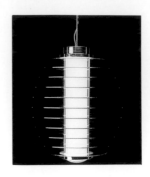

telephones can also be art, to the foreigners who think Italy is still living in the sixteenth century, to the Italians who don't want Italy to look like a cemetery of past glories."

Although with considerable delay, the Italians entered officially into the historical process of renewal in architecture at a very decisive moment. In fact, in that period the modern movement reached full maturity on an international level and realized, in a short time, some buildings that would be fundamental contributions to the history of architecture in the 20th century.

Only after 1930 did the group of Italian Rationalists advocate a general current towards simplification of styles and decoration, based on other European models, particularly those French and Austrian in origin. The Rationalists wished to transform overwrought, encrusted objects, as they had been designed so far, into modern objects in line with their functions, underlining the relationship between an object's basic shape and proportion on one hand, and purpose as well as its manufacturing methods on the other. However, though their ideas and projects, like so many pioneer works, challenged tradition-bound concepts, their proposals were still largely executed in the language from which they were trying to escape.

They still added to their projects a specific Italian touch, as an ideal continuity of the country's historical and stylistic tradition, in an effort to match modern machine civilization with what they saw as the best of western culture. Classical refinement, which had always been associated with Italian taste, became a characteristic in modern Italian industrial design as well.

With the common goal of bridging the technological gap, Italian design combined the heritage of a humanistic past with the newest technologies. Although with delay, the Italian designers showed from the start their skill in

producing objects of lasting elegance, immediately recognizable as the result of a particular taste and way of life. The upsurge toward a modern style was also commented on by official observers. In the journal, *Architettura e arti decorative,* Giovanni Papini wrote in 1925, "Today artists should not forget that we live in a period of simplification, a period of reaction against the excess of useless ornaments, against complicated line and forms."

Undoubtedly, furniture design was one of the fields in which the efforts by young Rationalist architects, whose designs were based on the principles of modernity, were more concentrated. Although by the end of the 1920s there were plenty of interesting projects, by Piero Bottoni, Gino Levi Montalcini, Giuseppe Pagano and Alberto Sartoris, for example, they did not get beyond the prototype stage because of the industrial backwardness of Italian furniture makers.

The occasion to see their projects produced on an industrial scale, although in limited series, came only through the erection of some major architectural works, such as the 1929 office building for the financier and art patron Gualino in Turin (by architects Levi Montalcini and Pagano), or the 1936 Montecatini building in Milan (for which, in addition to the building project, architect Giò Ponti designed part of the interior, including furniture, lighting and even restroom fixtures). Almost all project work in this field concerned supplies to public institutions. As to the materials, the use of steel facilitated standardization and mechanization of the manufacturing process and became popular for furniture for use in community buildings, hospitals, schools and factories. Metal furniture produced by the Parma company of Saronno, on the design by architects Albini and Pelanti, was purchased by the Italian Army, which, because of its light weight, solidity and easy assembly, used it widely in the African colonies.

However, as mentioned before, quantitatively, the impact was rather scarce.

Though contemporary magazines on architecture[2] gave extensive coverage to these new developments, the actual use of new materials was hardly ever applied to objects manufactured on a proper industrial scale. In general, handmade furniture still prevailed in the average family home. This was not surprising since the projects by Rationalist or *Novecento* avant-garde designers were acceptable only to wealthy and culturally open-minded customers and were, therefore, produced in limited numbers. In spite of the strong interest to launch the new materials and to promote an Italian style, design was still largely conditioned by the customs and the cultural level of the Italian public. Designers therefore tried to avoid the audacious innovations that might shock the consumer. In this period, the production of objects and furniture was still based on stable values, in consideration of the well-defined and unchanging social picture.

But then something started changing. On one side, through articles appearing in *Domus* and through displays at the Milan Triennales, architect Giò Ponti continued to pilot the taste of the upper middle class toward *handicrafted luxury*. On the other side, the same Ponti designed the *Domus Nova* series of accessibly priced furniture on sale in the department store La Rinascente and meant for widespread distribution. Architects also started tackling the field of fixed-furniture items, designing, for instance, bathroom and lavatory equipment. Giò Ponti worked for the Richard Ginori company in project supervision and image promotion; Ettore Sottsass, Sr. collaborated with Standard (today known as Ideal Standard).

It was in this period that some of the major manufacturers of artistic products decided to take a new course. Ceramica di Laveno found a precious and elegant collaborator in Guido Andloviz. In 1933, the Luigi Fontana Company entrusted Pietro Chiesa, Jr. with the artistic direction of their *Fontana Arte* division and with the design of their glass lamps and crystal objects.

In spite of the restrictions imposed by the fascist regime, those professionals who were not in line with the officially approved taste found opportunity to express their creative ideas in the field of interior design (not only for homes and offices, but also stores and art galleries), a branch usually neglected by party-supported architects. Architecture presented the problem of how to plan the living space, and it was therefore the task of architecture to define the new concepts for interior decoration, focusing not only on furniture, but on all the elements that make a home or work space livable: lighting equipment, household appliances, telephones and so on. Not by chance, it would be the achievements in interior decoration that, after the war, made Italian style famous all over the world, and that also largely contributed in drawing attention to Italian design in other fields.

An important opportunity in the field of household object design was offered by the great periodic exhibitions, primarily the Biennale in Monza, which continued as the *Triennale of decorative art and modern architecture* from 1927 to 1933. Throughout the 1920s and 1930s, the Triennale exhibitions were *the* meeting point for debate on what was then called *arti decorative* (or *arti industriali* depending on who was writing on it. The term *design* would not be used in Italy until the end of the 1940s). From its first editions of 1923, 1925 and 1927, this exhibition became a place of confrontation between form research, production and socio-political contexts, and gradually involved new groups of opinion and new branches of industry on the subject of design in different fields. Step by step, general thought opened up toward a new concep-

▶ View of the kitchen in the *Casa Elettrica* designed for the 4th Triennale exhibition of 1930 by Piero Bottoni.

tion of object creation. This led to concrete application of modern industrial design from the beginning of the 1950s onward.

The Triennale was unique among exhibitions because it allowed Italy to keep in touch with what was going on internationally in modern architecture through the hosting of foreign exhibitions and the introduction of foreign personalities. If the first two Triennales were still dominated by regional styles, the third exhibition, held in Monza in 1929, presented a totally different picture. Among the organizers were Margherita Sarfatti and Mario Sironi, both leading figures of the *Novecento* movement founded a year earlier. But at the 4th Monza exhibition in 1930, the tendency was clearly towards Rationalism. Also on display were appliances of the Berlin and Vienna Werkbund (*Deutscher* and *Wiener Werkbund*) with projects and products by Siemens, AEG and the Bauhaus.

The project of the *Casa Elettrica* (the electric home) carried out by Figini & Pollini for the Triennale of Monza, with furniture designed by Piero Bottoni, Guido Frette and Adalberto Libera, and sponsored by the Società Edison (the electricity company), was of great importance and somehow represented a physical manifesto of early Italian Rationalism. Actually, the *Casa Elettrica* exhibition housed, almost exclusively, electric household appliances manufactured abroad. The exhibition was meant to indicate a new way of development, offering a model for feasible future production. Although Italian contribution was limited, it was an important opportunity for confrontation by young architects, who followed with interest the development of new forms proposed in a concrete way by modern movements in other countries. Two years later, Figini & Pollini exhibited their own furniture creations at the Galleria del Milione in Milan.

For the 5th Triennale, the exhibition moved to

Milan, the "rising city" as Boccioni called it, the place of industrial wonders and business opportunities. Since then, the Triennale has had its own exhibition building in one of the Milan parks. From 1933, the exhibition was no longer generically named *of decorative arts* but *of modern decorative and industrial arts.* For those times, the new name had a programmatic and polemic quality. *Industrial* was added to accentuate the importance of technical efficiency in manufacturing and of mass production, and that the exhibition no longer focused only on unique pieces of craftsmanship. It further indicated that art also had its place in industrial production processes, as first Herbert Muthesius and later Walter Gropius had taught, and as was then being preached by the Italian Rationalists.

The change of seat (and name) coincided with the definitive national and international recognition of the Triennale's importance. Most of the credit went to Giò Ponti, its principal animator and organizer. His efforts were aimed at collecting, in one large avant-garde exhibition, a variety of experimental products of uneven value, all equally oriented towards a new way of designing.

This fifth exhibition was no doubt the most significant and clamorous of that period, since it was the meeting point as well as battle field of the two most dynamic trends of the moment: Neoclassicism and Rationalism. The dispute concerned in particular their differing ideas about modern home design. This Triennale housed an international show on modern architecture, with 40 full-scale models of villas and low-income, one-family houses erected in the park, designed by such names as Le Corbusier, Gropius, Frank Lloyd Wright, Mies van der Rohe, Adolf Loos and Erich Mendelsohn. The effect was remarkable; some were enthusiastic about the modernity and novelty, many were scandalized and irritated. But it would also be the last great exhibition on an international level to

► The 1936 Triennale included an exhibition of design from Finland, featuring the bentwood furniture of Alvar Aalto.

be held under the fascist regime. Italy's cultural relations with other countries were doomed to gradually come to an end.

In spite of the violent polemics, but also thanks to the shock provoked, the cultural atmosphere underwent a definite change after 1933, not so much owing to architecture or the other *noble* arts, as to the time of greater maturity and considerable development witnessed in interior decoration, decorative and graphic art. This was evidenced by the new interiors of shops, bars, restaurants, the new aggressive colors and styles in advertising, by the search for sometimes openly surrealistic or abstract solutions, that only a few years earlier would have met with general disapproval. Also, modern art was exuberant and booming and, among its other supremacies, Milan became Italy's number one city for art exhibitions and the marketplace for modern art. Cultural and artistic life in Milan was, of course, also stimulated by the presence of such literary personalities as Riccardo Bacchelli, Massimo Bontempelli, Guido Piovene, Salvatore Quasimodo, and committed critics such as Pier Maria Bardi, Giuseppe Pagano, Edoardo Persico and Raffaele Carrieri.

In 1935, the League of Nations condemned the Italian aggression in Abyssinia and decided to adopt sanctions against fascist Italy. The regime reacted by stepping out of the League of Nations; Germany and, paradoxically, the Soviet Union were the only countries that continued to supply arms to Italy. The regime also created a climate of siege, although Italy's economy was only slightly affected. More serious were the cultural consequences; as war rhetoric was getting more hysterical, most intellectuals started turning their backs on fascism, which soon could only count on a few "zealous idiots"[2]

The *autarchy* (national production in the name of economic self-sufficiency) was proclaimed. Besides the

use of curved steel tube, almost an emblem of modern design, the experimentation and use of new *autarkic* materials was encouraged. Some of these materials were: securit glass, moldrite, anticorodal (an aluminium alloy), faesite, as well as linoleum and buxus for floor covering and paneling.

Due to the changed political situation, foreign participation at the 6th Triennale (1936) was very scarce, with the important exception of an exhibition of works by Alvar Aalto, introducing Finnish design to the Italian public. This Triennale, headed by architect Giuseppe Pagano, was meant by the curators to be the consecration of Italian Rationalism in all fields, but instead it coincided with the first signs of the crisis. In the following years, the Rationalists were gradually ousted when it came to commissions of important state-controlled architectural projects and, consequently, ignored in the official cultural debate channelled through the regime's media. The regime's cultural organs favored a revival of the mythical splendor of ancient Rome. The risk of a return to academic principles became evident.

The problem was not only political. The blind belief in Rationalism was waning and, after the long fight for modernity, more weight was again given to free and imaginative invention, with heightened attention to ornamentation.

With the Spanish Civil War and the later anti-Semitic campaigns, the political situation was getting darker. At the inauguration of the 7th Triennale, Europe was already overrun by the war. Orthodox Rationalism still found qualified supporters; one of the topics of the exhibition was the necessity to change the process of *designing* an object into a proper methodology closely related to industrial processes. This involved the difficult task of reconciling the apparently antagonist concepts of individuality (the artist,

► The Fiat 508 Balilla, introduced in 1932, was the company's first "economy" car. Three body types were offered, equipped with a three-speed manual transmission.

architect or craftsman) and standardization (industry), and of creating closer collaboration between artist and manufacturer for their mutual benefit. Arguments about the role of the architect and the artist in the quickly changing conditions of the new century were common.

The main issue concerned the problem of standardization. Although handmade objects could have (and usually do have) variations, industry could not work in this manner. It was not just a matter of aesthetic principles, but also of cultural and social significance. Such objects were displayed for the first time at the International Exhibition of Mass Production, curated by Pagano, and covered various categories, from office equipment by Marcello Nizzoli to radio sets by the Castiglionis.

A more thorough examination of the various fields of production gives a better idea of the impact of industrial design in Italy in those times. In fact, after 1930, many of the ideas and many of the personalities that would make Italian design world-known in the years to come had already emerged. This first decade already saw the characteristics of the later development of Italian style: sensitivity and imagination in research, prompt reaction to the cultural and functional requirements of a wide variety of products, from household goods to means of transportation, from simple tools to industrial machinery. The weak points also became evident: a still rather restricted market, lack of money in large parts of the population, hesitation and cultural narrow-mindedness or even diffidence toward innovation in the middle class.

In spite of this, in some important branches, such as aeronautic design, Italy was already outstanding. But here the idea was to create exclusive, and thus of limited production, models fit for great performance that the whole world would envy. Priority was therefore given to the production of the double-wing hydroplane, a construc-

tion which became popular in civil aviation, whereas most other types of aircraft were either imported or built on license. The same pattern applied to the automobile industry, which aimed at producing glamorous cars mainly for export, whereas the home market was discovered only in 1932 when Fiat brought out the *Balilla 508,* the first car to be sold at an accessible price.

The railways, nationalized since 1905, operated as a monopoly and were therefore relatively independent from the rules of the market. This obviously reflected on industrial design. Closed to any suggestion from the outside and accustomed to doing their own planning of the rolling stock up to the smallest detail, the technical offices of the railways left no margin for initiative to the manufacturers. In 1933, a first attempt was made to entrust architects with the interior design of trains; the details of the internal furnishing of a railway coach were designed for the Breda factory by Ponti and Pagano. The model was shown at the 5th Triennale, but also in this case, the limits imposed on the designers were very narrow.

The year 1932 saw the appearance of the *Littorina* (its name derived from Mussolini's inaugural journey between Rome and Littoria, one of the newly founded towns under the régime), a railroad motor coach with incorporated combustion engine. Almost 250 coaches of this model were put into service throughout Italy between the years 1933 and 1940. Its streamlined body, its large windows and its high speed of 140 Km/h—almost twice as fast as the locomotives of the time—represented a jump into the future to the average Italian.

Among the technical novelties that started having wide distribution, the telephone and the wireless were considered status symbols. While the telephone was associated with a certain modern and wealthy style of life, the radio became one of fascism's means for mass propa-

► Franco Albini's transparent radio of 1938 shattered notions of how a radio should look.

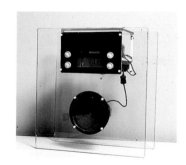

ganda. The technological innovations of the early 1930s allowed the reduction of the dimensions of the massive containers that had so far determined their image. On the occasion of the 5th Triennale exhibition, *Domus* magazine, together with the *Società Internazionale del Grammofono,* launched a contest for the design of a radio grammophone, which was won by Figini & Pollini. For the following Triennale, in 1936, another contest by *Domus* invited the participants to use preferably Italian materials (with a clear hint to Italian autarchy). At the 7th Triennale, an entire exhibition, organized by Luigi Caccia Dominioni, together with Livio and Pier Giacomo Castiglioni, concerned the wireless set.

The traditional form of the cumbersome radio cabinet was abandoned to make way for a new shape which did not hide the technical aspects, but gave more scope to the radio's actual function. Giuseppe Bianchini, chairman of the 7th Triennale, wrote in his presentation of the catalog, ''This exhibition on wireless sets is meant to show the public and the manufacturers that radio sets can and must have much better and handsomer shapes and details than the radio industry has so far offered. Patient selection and continuous evolution will result in a radio set of a typical form in line with what has been achieved for other instruments that have by now found a place in our homes (telephone, piano).''

Among the Italian industries, Olivetti in particular was very open to the application of industrial design. Founded in 1908 by Camillo Olivetti, the company was directed from 1933 by his son Adriano. The aim was to conquer new markets for the versatile and handy Olivetti machines and, at the same time, to strengthen the firm's global image through modern design, not only of its products and advertising materials, but also of its showrooms, office and industrial buildings. To this purpose, the graphic

art portion was commissioned to designers Costantino Nivola, Giovanni Pintori and Xanti Schawinsky and the building projects to architects Figini & Pollini. In 1929, a new projects office was opened. In 1931, the company's first portable typewriter, designed by Ing. Marelli, appeared on the market, to be followed in 1935 by the *Studio 42* model, the successful result of efficient teamwork by engineer Luzzati, architects Figini & Pollini and advertising expert Schawinsky. From that moment on, collaboration between technicians and artists became a characteristic feature of the Olivetti production. Besides technical research, form design became an important factor, and continuous efforts were made to combine, in an efficient and harmonious way, the body of the machine and its mechanical parts in order to obtain an aesthetic product, in line with avant-garde ideas of a truly *modern* way of life. In 1940, Olivetti presented its first calculating machine, the *Multisumma,* designed by architect Marcello Nizzoli.

Notes

[1] ''Rassegna italiana,'' *Architettura,* December 1926; ''Gli stranieri,'' *Architettura* February 1927; ''Impreparazione-incompresione-pregiudizi,'' *Architettura* March 1927; ''Una nuova epoca arcaica,'' *Architettura* May 1927.

[2] In those years, specialized magazines started playing a role of growing importance. *Domus,* founded and edited by Giò Ponti (1928), followed by *Casabella* and *Poligono* (1929), *Edilizia Moderna* and *Quadrante* (1933/35), provided punctual reviews of new projects and materials and amply reported on the evolution of the decorative arts.

The 1940s

The world conflict left Italy's economy exhausted. Although the industries were less heavily destroyed than in other countries, the war damages to transport infrastructures and built areas were enormous.

The technical gap between Italy and the rest of Europe and, above all, the United States—concealed by fascist propaganda up to and during the war—became fully evident after the defeat. Vast areas, especially in the south, seemed doomed to chronic depression, whereas in the rest of the peninsula, urbanization and industrial development had started, prevailing on what had been a rural and agricultural society.

Post-war reconstruction and reconversion were to bring the country back on the international scene. In spite of a lack of government planning and the large number of enterprises with state participation, production and national income soon showed conspicuous and constant increases. This was largely stimulated by the proverbial Italian capacity for improvisation, particularly in the small and medium industries which were doing their best to catch up with modern technology, giving special care to the styling of their products.

Architects and designers participated in this evolution, well aware of the tight relationship between architecture, industry and politics, where their proposals might have been of crucial importance. This required close collaboration within all fields of production. In a conference of 1946[1], Ernesto Nathan Rogers, trying to define the architect/designer's field of operation, invented the slogan that was to become famous, *Dal cucchiaio alla città* (From spoon to city). Since it was based on the same principles as architectural design, the designer's work could encompass any type of product, whatever its dimensions or function.

The austerity of the war period was followed by an explosion of creativity which went hand in hand with the demand for products that were beautiful and, at the same time, affordable. Before the war, only a few industries availed themselves of the work of a designer, but then he became a figure of growing importance in creating a reliable image of the product, and thus of its manufacturer.

Besides the founders and pioneers of Italian industrial design (Nizzoli, Ponti, Albini, Carlo Mollino), a second generation of designers was coming up (for instance, the Castiglionis and Marco Zanuso). Some of them had made their first steps forward at the pre-war Triennale exhibitions.

The countless small factories in northern Italy, based on a solid background of artisan craftsmanship, were being modernized with new industrial structures, creating a fertile soil for Italian design. This allowed the designer to work in a situation where the manufacturers were willing to spend money on the research of new forms and materials, but to also take the risk of experimenting with new ideas that sometimes seemed contrary to the current market demand.

Besides the renowned entrepreneurs who had created industrial empires, such as Olivetti or Pirelli, there were numerous small producers, ex-factory workers skilled at the turning lathe and able to resolve the technical and production problems in their own businesses. This type of manufacturer knew nothing about artistic currents and could not be bothered with the social aspects of the product, but recognized an attractive object when he saw one and immediately figured what market it might have.

The Italian designers found, in this class of industrialists, men with an open ear for even the most unconventional proposals, ready to invest and, above all, keen to try them out. Thus, many objects that otherwise would have been considered avant-garde had the chance to become mass-produced, allowing the consumer to buy a sewing machine featuring utility combined with culture. This fortunate blend of interests would result in the typical image of goods made in Italy.

The basic characteristics of Italian design were emerging: talent, persevering effort and experimentation. Proud and slightly boastful about their creative work, the Italians went in for wide publicity. Italy has always been the country with the highest number of magazines on architecture, design and interior decoration, mostly of high quality and with large circulations. Their readership not being confined to insiders only, these publications fulfilled the double task of molding the taste of the general public and keeping specialists *au courant* with the latest trends. The leading magazine in this field was *Domus* (founded and edited by Giò Ponti from 1928 to 1940 and again from 1948 until his death in 1979, with a brief but important interlude by E. N. Rogers from 1946 to 1948).

As prior to the war, it was the furniture industry where the collaboration between designer and producer was strongest. Housing projects totaling fifteen million rooms to build (and to furnish) represented an enormous potential market. Already in 1946, an exhibition was inaugurated in Milan (in the same *Palazzo dell'Arte* which had housed the pre-war Triennales), organized by RIMA (*Riunione Italiana Mostre di Arredamento*), on furniture for wide distribution, with emphasis on the products' "economy, functionality, good taste." The exhibition also envisaged mass production, but here the main issue was of a theoretical and moral nature; the objects had to be "democratic" (within everybody's reach), whereas their practical and aesthetic features were of secondary importance.

One year later, the Milan Triennale took up its role again as a showcase of the results achieved by combined experimentation and manufacturing. The topics of the 8th Triennale (1947), the first one after the war, concerned Italian reconstruction, in particular the building industry and furniture for the masses. Besides showing furniture and objects for daily use designed for mass production, the exhibition still reserved quite some space for artisan handicraft, but the main issue was to show a modern way of designing to resolve the housing problem.

In other areas of Italy's industry, the looks of a product became more and more important. Emblematic for the reconversion of war industry was the case of Piaggio. Specialized since 1917 in the designing and building of airplanes, in the 1930s this enterprise was comprised of various plants for naval equipment and railway coaches, and, during the last years of the war, four of its factories produced aircraft. In 1946, using a surplus of starting motors for planes, Piaggio began the production of a revolutionary scooter (a completely new version of the traditional motorbike), the *Vespa*. The rapidly improving standard of living allowed the masses to get motorized, at first on two wheelers such as the *Vespa* or the *Lambretta* (the latter made by Innocenti, which formerly produced piping material), before switching over to automobiles. In those years, Fiat, whose production concentrated on small- and medium-sized cars, strengthened its predominant position, capturing as much as 92–93 percent of the entire Italian automobile market in 1956.

In 1946, Dante Giacosa, who had contributed to the design of the famous *Cisitalia* automobile, became Fiat's project manager. While Fiat became a monopoly in the production of economical automobiles, Lancia and Alfa Romeo continued to specialize in luxury cars. With the increasing output of Italian cars, the fame of Italian coachwork design spread rapidly. In other fields, collaboration between design and industry was still rather limited, except for the first endeavors made in modular kitchen

► The ETR 300 electric train was designed in 1947 by Giulio Minoletti for Breda Ferroviaria.

and bathroom furniture, bookcases and metal wall racks, which were nothing new compared to already existing foreign products.

A case apart was Olivetti, which since the 1930s had always been a pioneer in launching well-designed articles and seized the opportunity for a period of expansion, culminating in 1959 with the creation of the *ELEA 9000,* the first computer completely designed in Italy. Under the management of Adriano Olivetti, the company developed a business philosophy so far unequaled in Italy. In fact, in building its plants, designed in collaboration with the Nizzoli studio, Olivetti not only considered the mere requirements of the manufacturing process, but also saw to it that the building fit efficiently and harmoniously in the environmental and social context, providing the factory area with services such as nurseries, libraries, community centers and housing. Integrated design helped to create a united image for all of the company's aspects. Olivetti products, houses for Olivetti personnel, Olivetti advertising material—everything was studied with the same care. In 1946, the company brought out the *Lexicon 80* designed by Nizzoli, the first typewriter to be exhibited at the Museum of Modern Art in New York. A company news letter stated, ''. . . what interests Nizzoli mainly is weighing the largest number of possibilities, now working out a given scheme to the last detail, now comparing it with others already sketched and then collecting the most positive points the design already executed can provide . . . . it is not unusual for the form to improve progressively but to reveal some degree of incompatibility with the mechanism that it is to contain. In following the the interior logic of a plastic form, Nizzoli, to a certain extent, has to accept the consequences. And these do not always correspond to the contribution of the mechanical parts. In such cases, all he can do is ask for a change in the arrangement of the

machine. His request has only a slight chance of being satisfied, requiring, as it often must, a long and costly, if not inadvisable or impossible, replanning. His work accordingly has to start again, more or less from scratch.''[2]

Notes

[1] *Domus,* n. 215, November 1946
[2] P. C. Santini, ''Marcello Nizzoli, designer,'' *Notizie Olivetti,* n. 71, Milan, April 1971

The 1950s

The early 1950s were crucial years for the evolution of Italian design. Thanks to the country's industrial development, more and more fields of production opened up to the collaboration of designers, in particular for sophisticated goods, such as machine tools, automobiles, electrical household appliances and precision instruments. Throughout the 1950s, the designers' work remained based on a very homogeneous formula. Object design was aimed at creating a product whose form suited its purpose; its style had to match its utility and functionality. The object was unambiguously seen as an article that had to face the market, but care given to its qualities of performance did not imply subordination to strict economic considerations.

The designer's competence also consisted of distinguishing between the consumers' real needs and those artificially created by the market to sell superfluous goods. The real value and dignity of his work was based on the ethical principle of refusing to comply with the consumers' bad or kitschy taste, and also of refusing to accept the manufacturer's pressure to give the product a new look when redesigning its form was not called for by technical or functional necessity, but only by marketing attempts toward a more saleable item.

The original characteristics were becoming evident in Italian industrial design. Considered a synthesis between production and culture, it was the result of creative collaboration in which the designer was not influenced by fads or market trends, but could follow his own taste and technical insight, and thus have an important role in determining the final product.

"American design represents one of the results of a system of free competition in which particular economic and productive conditions have led to continuous expansions of the markets and consequently improved product quality."[1] In the case of Italy, the designer became a leading element within the industrial process, with the capacity to suggest and influence trends of development.

Companies were founded that would become famous for their contribution to the transformation of Italian furniture: Kartell (1949) with an influential role in the design of plastic objects; Arflex (1950) linked to Pirelli; Gavina (1953); and Tecno (1954).

In other fields, various manufacturing firms started industrial production with the contribution of famous architects. For example, Solari began collaboration with the BBPR studio and Gino Valle for the design of clocks and flap-unit display boards, while Brionvega worked with Marco Zanuso for the design of radio and television sets.

Using new technologies and materials largely imported from other countries, Italian industries soon modernized and the designers exploited the possibilities offered by these new substances and production methods, elaborating them to create objects with completely new forms and functions that differed from those initially planned. Inspired by techniques already experimented with in automobile interiors, Zanuso designed furniture of foam rubber and *Nastricord.* The Castiglionis, among others, developed the concept of *ready-made* through the functional transposition of traditional materials and techniques presented in a new spirit.

In 1951, the 9th Triennale presented the exhibition *Le forme dell'utile* (Utilitarian forms), and the Milan Trade Fair of 1952 included a panorama on *Arte ed estetica industriale,* followed one year later by a second presentation on the same topic, *Seconda mostra dell'estetica industriale.* In 1953, Olivetti presented a display of its products and graphic design at New York's Museum of Modern Art. That same year, *Domus* announced that an association of industrial designers had been founded through the initiative of Romualdo Borletti, owner of the department

◀ The Lettera 22 portable typewriter was introduced by Olivetti in 1950. Designed by Marcello Nizzoli, the compact typewriter was a revolutionary concept.

store La Rinascente, Adriano Olivetti, Mario Revelli, Ernesto Rogers and Marco Zanuso. The founding corporate sponsors were Fiat, Montecatini, Olivetti and Pirelli.

The editors of *Domus* undertook the task of issuing a multilingual yearbook with an up-to-date directory of the Italian industrial designers stating, "This is the moment of industrial design not only for what it means in terms of taste and aesthetics of industrial products, but also because of its importance for culture and technique, for civilization and tradition, for home furnishing and for the building industry, above all, for our country whose raw material and vocation has always been (and with God's help always will be) creating things of beauty."[2]

There was a revival of the desire to combine scientific and humanistic culture with the subtle balance between these two components that is typical of the best of Italian design. In 1954, the Compasso d'Oro was created, a prize to award industrialists and designers excelling in the search for the best "aesthetic quality and technical and functional characteristics of industrial products". The fact that the prize was promoted by a large department store such as La Rinascente meant that the market was by now attaching great importance to good design. In the following years, the choices made by the jury for the Compasso d'Oro indicated the evolution of design within the marketplace during Italy's major period of economic development.

Also in 1954, among the many existing specialized design publications, a new magazine appeared. The topics of *Stile industria* were industrial design, graphics and packaging. Besides up-to-date information, it contained historical and critical contributions, theoretical articles and debates. For nearly ten years (until its last issue in 1963), it would be a precious working instrument and forum.

The year 1954 also saw the 10th Triennale, exhibiting 150 objects from all over the world in its *Mostra internazionale dell'industrial design*. The emphasis was on the relationship between art and industrial production, whereas less space was reserved for the products' technical and commercial aspects and for artisan production, which had still dominated previous exhibitions. At the same moment, a convention was held by the Triennale's *Centro Studi* on the connections between design and society and of the role of the designer. Max Bill defined the spirit of the convention, saying, "The purpose of any object must be to serve man, and as all men together form our society, these objects have an important function in social human life." If on one side, the objects selected by the Triennale, due to their cost and style, were intended for an élite, on the other side, the products awarded at the first edition of the Compasso d'Oro included features that could make them popular with a much wider audience. Besides Nizzoli's portable Olivetti *Lettera 22* typewriter, there was the *48 AL* automatic rifle manufactured by Franchi, which would eventually sell over one million pieces, and the *BU* sewing machine, designed by Nizzoli for Necchi, also a mass-market item.

In 1956, the ADI (*Associazione per il Disegno Industriale*) was founded, consisting of roughly ninety product and graphic designers as well as manufacturers. The first meeting was held in Giò Ponti's studio. Through the years, the association became steadily more important, although the names that appeared on the jury and among the Compasso d'Oro winners were always the same. In fact, in 1957 the organization of the Compasso d'Oro award was taken over by the ADI.

The 25th Milan Trade Fair comprised a *Mostra internazionale per l'estetica delle materie plastiche* on the styling of plastic materials, following the successes obtained by Italian research work (Giulio Natta had been awarded

The 1956 Fiat 500 was designed by Dante Giacosa. It improved upon the original 500 series, incorporating such features as rear-engine drive and independent suspension.

the Nobel prize for Chemistry) and by Italy's chemical industry in the fields of technopolymers and synthetic resins. The production of plastic materials between 1959 and 1963 had increased fifteenfold. At the same time, the designers showed a growing interest in these new materials that allowed them to combine in a simple and functional form the ideology of *Equalitarian Rationalism* (mass production of equal objects for equal men) and the requirements of creative projection. The new plastics offered seemingly endless possibilities of application in almost any field, including furniture.

In 1957, the 11th Triennale housed the umpteenth *Mostra internazionale di industrial design,* the last one of its kind until the 16th edition. Polemics arose from those who saw industrial design as a servant of capital, reiterating opinions already expressed by various participants at the convention of 1954.

At that occasion, the well-known critic Giulio Carlo Argan forecasted the evolution of the role of designer from "exponent of a technical bourgeoisie," to "exponent of the working class, of those who make the product," thus resolving "the problem of the conflict between capitalism and labor."

The period saw Italian intellectuals turn further to the left, with the tendency to shoot at anything that gave them a living. And they were backed up by some manufacturers who were anxious to assure their own future. There was also a change in style. Design, "renouncing direct reference, on the narrow relationship between function and the human anatomy, expands into more abstract forms. We may assume that there is no longer the urgency of functional justification which was the reason for breaking away from traditionally styled design. We are, therefore, approaching other forms of styling with such seductive features that we may already now foresee the

risk of mannerism in the coming years."[3]

The late 1950s witnessed the development of what in Italy was called the *Neoliberty* style (neo art nouveau), adopted by architects such as the Castiglionis, Joe Colombo, Vittorio Gregotti and Vico Magistretti. It was a formal innovation that may be seen as an ironic refusal of Rationalist functionalism, leading to the developments of the 1960s.

Notes

[1] Alberto Rosselli, "Incontro alla realtà", *Stile e industria,* n. 3, January 1955

[2] *Domus,* n. 269, 1953

[3] Angelo Tito Anselmi, "L'industrial design alla Triennale", *Civiltà delle macchine,* Sept.–Nov. 1957

▼ The Selene chair was designed in 1968 by Vico Magistretti. Produced by Artemide, the stackable chair is made of molded plastic resin.

The 1960s

In the 1960s, Italy reached the peak of its economic boom. An unprecedented increase of domestic consumption was achieved, thanks to higher purchasing power in a large part of the population. Italian design was still living through its golden period, though there were premonitory signs of a malaise because of the designers' difficulties in defining their professional role in a rapidly evolving society. But dissent was still subdued; the economy was doing well, there was work for all and little time for abstract theorizing.

In those years, many typical forms that had always been associated with particular objects, and thus with particular functions, were revolutionized by the use of new materials and new production techniques. Such was the case with electronic devices and the miniaturization of their various components. But the strongest impact came from plastic materials, especially technopolymers. Their use was soon expanding, owing to the decisive contributions by some of the main producers (Pirelli, Montecatini, Anic, ENI) to perform research in the industrial design field. These studies investigated the new possibilities offered by plastics through redesign of traditional objects and elaboration of new forms based on the specific properties of the new materials.

Until then, plastics still had the image of a *poor* material and were mostly used for inexpensive, often disposable articles. The intervention of industrial design changed this situation; plastics were no longer considered surrogates for more precious materials—such as wood, metal, crystal with their higher costs and proven durability—but were now appreciated for their intrinsic qualities: low manufacturing costs, ductility, resistance, light weight and a large assortment of colors.

Plastics were immediately and successfully applied in the furniture industry. The use of injection-molded plastics made it possible to produce items of furniture that no longer had the slightest relationship with the traditional skills and concerns of cabinetmaking. Objects that had been thought unchangeable acquired completely new forms; for example, the object *chair*[1], which sometimes totally lost its familiar original features by which most chairs could be identified, such as seat, back, legs and arms. Already in 1963, the most important company in this field, Kartell, produced an injection-molded polyethene child's chair designed by Marco Zanuso and Richard Sapper, and in 1967, the *Model 4869* designed by Joe Colombo, while in 1968, Artemide introduced the *Selene*, a design by Vico Magistretti.

Of course, as happens with all novelties, there was soon excessive use of plastic materials. Within the following decade, however, the resulting abuses would be redimensioned by the oil crisis, which forced a return to so-called natural materials.

The use of flexible polyurethane foams allowed one to experiment with innovative shapes for furniture. In some cases, the padding prevailed over the frame, which was hidden inside the body. This seating type soon became very popular and formed a separate category of furniture called *gli imbottiti* (the padded).

Another aspect of this period was the invention (and also the eventual excess) of modular furniture for home or office. Low cost and greater formal and functional adaptability assisted in the success of this furniture type, made of elements that are, at the same time, containers and partition walls, whose ideological origin can be traced back to concepts beloved by the protagonists of the modern movement.

At the beginning of the century, small household or office appliance designs tended to reveal their mechanical complexity or, on the contrary, the mechanism was reas-

suringly concealed in a traditionally shaped container. Sewing machines, for instance, would display most of their moving parts and connections, each part articulated as a distinct shape. Radio sets were instead disguised as pieces of furniture whose shapes were not determined by technical considerations, but only by factors of taste.

Though most of our mechanical appliances today have a shell or package protecting and concealing the machinery within, their form is characteristic and unmistakable. But while refrigerators, vacuum cleaners, toasters, sewing machines or radios have begun to resemble each other, not all are necessarily anonymous containers. Many industrial designers have successfully avoided arbitrary shapes, while at the same time emphasizing a certain object's functional parts so that its very form suggests its correct use. The designers of the 1960s started emphasizing some functional elements in the hull of the objects they created. For instance, in the radio sets, the knobs and the loudspeaker were pointed out, as in those designed in the years 1965–66 by Marco Zanuso, Richard Sapper and the Castiglioni brothers for Brionvega.

Surprisingly, the most successful period of Italian design (In 1961, the board of the Milan Trade Fair, recognizing the growing international importance of the Italian furniture industry, held its first trade exhibition in this field, the *Salone del Mobile Italia*.) coincided with a crisis of the very institutions that had most helped to promote it. The ADI (Association of Italian Design) had remained a kind of exclusive designers' club, whose members, year after year, took their turn on the jury of the Compasso d'Oro prize in order to honor one another. Hidden behind objectives of exclusive cultural importance, the association avoided realistic consideration of the commercial aspects of industrially produced objects. The ADI missed the opportunity of becoming an organ through which effective

▶ Marco Zanuso designed the ST 201, 12-inch screen television set in 1968. The set, manufactured by Brionvega, has a black, transparent metacrylate exterior.

contact with industry might promote the application of design in the many fields of manufacturing where it was still ignored.

The Compasso d'Oro award was itself in a crisis. Until then, the prize-winning works had been self-contained objects, since their production remained rather occasional and reserved for an élite. From 1962 on, more consideration was given to marketing aspects as the prize-winning designs soon became the models for and image of high-quality mass production. In spite of this positive trend, in 1963, when the magazine *Stile Industria* closed down due to economic problems, the editor, drawing on the balance of recent experiences, wrote in the last issue, "the position of the industrial designer is today the topic of a dispute between the interests of industry and those of culture, and there is still a wide gap between them."[2]

The following year, at the 8th edition of the Compasso d'Oro, the jury's report underlined the usual problems which by now seemed to have become chronic. The summary of deficiencies listed included: "the designer being often used as a consultant kept outside the manufacturing process; the scarce participation in the debate on design in Italy by the decision makers; the almost total lack of specific schools for future-designers; the exiguity of exchanges and information; the fact that many fields are sliding towards the *neostylistic* phase of modern formalism." A process of self-analysis and self-criticism set in, which would reach its peak immediately after the upheavals of 1968.

The Triennale, owing to its excellent exhibitions, had long been an important reference point, but in the 1960s was no longer willing to give any space to autonomous shows on industrial design. It also renounced definitely the idea of presenting exhibitions of commercial products, by then made superfluous by the specialized fairs of the

Salone del Mobile and *Eurodomus*. But the Triennale was not able to propose for itself a new, articulate role. It should have taken the themes and "problems" treated in its previous editions, collecting them into one coherent trend, as had been done before the war when the Triennale had propagated the Rationalist proposals. But there was no longer a clear trend of ideas as had been the case earlier. The debates of the convention held during the 1960 Triennale still centered on the old topic of how to define the relationship between artist and designer and between artisan and industrial production.

The 13th Triennale (1964) was just as anachronistic with its focus on the theme "leisure time," considering the economic boom was over and recession had begun. In fact, after 1963, Italy's economy not only failed to expand at its 1950s rhythm, but actually dropped below the levels it had already reached. In any case, this edition of the Triennale was considered a turning point of Italian design. The *leitmotiv* "leisure time" was only a pretext to present the choices and trends of many young designers who would become leading figures in later years. The accent was on the notion of physical environment in all its complexity and on the designer's task to attempt to regulate the relationship that each object has with the rest of reality. The idea of environmental control was a point of issue, though nothing guaranteed that the sum of individually well-designed products could in any way help to resolve the problem of a degrading environment.

While Italy's intricate political lobby system was continuously shaken by scandals, the second half of the 1960s witnessed an accentuation of social conflicts. As the international economic crisis got more dramatic, left-wing parties and unions gained more political importance. The situation culminated in the revolt of students and intellectuals in 1960 and the massive strikes in the *hot autumn*

► The RR 126 stereo system was designed
by Achille and Pier Giacomo Castiglioni in
1964 for Brionvega.

of 1969. These events also expressed the malaise of the middle class, who, for the first time since the war, had to face menacing unemployment and the prospect of a lower standard of living.

Many involved with industrial design started complaining that, in the frantic rush for consumption, the social aspect of design, considered one of its foremost features, had been totally left in the background. Left-wing rhetoric always had many followers in the design profession and, in the years just before 1968, the idea had taken root that, due to his condition of being *exploited,* the designer really was in the same boat as the labor class, since within the logic of industrial production there was no scope for his creative capacities and, consequently, no guarantee for his survival in periods of economic crisis. The shifting to the left-wing ideology was well commented on by the critic Giulio Carlo Argan, who in 1967 stated that "designers can adopt a critical attitude towards the system" by separating "from the privileged class of industrial technicians," and eventually joining the "disinherited class of the intellectuals".[3] Many seemed convinced that the new techniques of environmental and community design would give them a chance to overcome the frustrating limitations imposed by collaboration with capitalism, exclusively based on production and consumption. But these expectations would prove largely unsubstantiated. Orders for public works by official institutions, who ideally act for the common good, were not coming forward to replace commissions from private enterprises. Opportunities to participate in urban development plans would be scarce for many years to come. One of the few exceptions was the offer to a team of Milan designers (architects Franco Albini and Franca Helg, graphic designer Bob Noorda) to create the image of the Milan underground transport (the first line was inaugurated in 1964).

At that time, however, there appeared to be many viable alternative proposals, and the very basis on which industrial design had so far been founded were being put into discussion. A critic commented, "I find it difficult to recognize a link between the requirements of the manufacturers, which are those of ever higher sales, of simplification of the manufacturing processes, of technical and technological improvement, of a so-called scientific experimentation (or even invention), that are all based on the parameter of consumption and thus on the consumer's degree of receptiveness; and on the other end, the requirements of those involved in designing claiming priority for invention and creativity . . . The aspect of communication . . . must assume priority over other components of its use such as functional, technical or economical parameters . . ."[4]

At the very moment that Italian design had succeeded in consolidating its undiscussed international supremacy, it was surprisingly put at stake by a minority of Italian designers who, in an effort to get into the limelight (in which they succeeded), launched two successive subversive movements, Radical Design, and Memphis. This paradoxical situation was, however, a symptom of the need for linguistic renewal and of the crisis of ideas and ideals in the entire field with its traditional values derived from the Rationalist culture. It was the first indication of real uneasiness caused by a loss of ideology, security, unitary vision and universally recognized critical parameters. Utopian projects and conceptual objects were being devised to highlight the reversal of values and the abolition of dogmas that were stylistically obsolete. The cult of production and consumption was seen as self-destructive, as the annihilation not only of social values, but also of environment itself, which appeared to be irreparably damaged. There was a rejection of technical progress and a return to

◄ De Pas, D'Urbino, Lomazzi, Scolari
designed the inflatable Blow armchair for
Zanotta in 1967.

symbolic, archaic and artisan forms of production, or alternatively, one's knowledge was put at the service of political activities.

Until the end of the 1960s, the products of design, although never of a homogeneous character, were still usually identifiable as Italian. The loss of a common cultural line resulted in a vehement debate, while the unitary image of Italian design was doomed to disappear rapidly. The crisis of the modern movement, with its reassuring certainties, occurred parallel with the discovery of a chaotic, vulgar, but in spite of this, not less rich or fascinating world. There was some talk of "anti-design" in an endeavor to reform, but this refuge into utopia was most likely due as much to a crisis of ideals as to a lack of commissioned work in a difficult economic period.

Already by the end of the 1950s, in the area between art and design, there had been a trend in England and Austria to break away from functionalist dogmas. The English, with such groups as Archigram and Street Farmer, recovered the language of the mass-media, from comic strips to advertising, with many aspects common to pop-art. Others, for example Hans Hollein (who in 1962 elaborated his anti-functionalist manifesto), sought inspiration in German-expressionist architecture. The situation led to the rise of Radical Design (also known as Antidesign, Counterdesign, Design Povero, etc.). Started in Italy by Ettore Sottsass, Jr. (without however effecting his "serious" work at Olivetti, which was still conducted with traditional methods), the new current immediately took different directions according to the personalities of its leading figures, such as Ugo La Pietra, Andrea Branzi and Alessandro Mendini in Milan, Gaetano Pesce in Venice, and the Archizoom and Superstudio groups in Florence. Their performances hardly ever went beyond the creation of prototypes. Besides, real production of these objects "with a

poetic function"[5] was never seriously contemplated, not even by the designers themselves.

Radical Design denounced the alleged connivances of design in the capitalist system. It propagated the refusal to develop the relationship with the commercial and technological reality of industry. Rather than with the product, the Radical designers seemed to feel more at ease with a project that remained at the stage of a drawing or even a written document. But they did find ample publicity for their creations in *Domus* from 1967 to 1972, and then until 1976 in *Casabella,* both directed in those periods by a Radical Design leader, Alessandro Mendini. Radical Design turned out mostly unfeasible projects, but also some amusing commercial products, such as the bean bag and the inflatable armchairs (*Sacco* and *Blow*) or the *Valentina* typewriter, apparently designed for picnicking poets[6]. In spite of the limited impact of its propositions, Radical Design had a certain importance insofar as it influenced the further developments of Italian design. "It encouraged investigating and coming to terms with bad taste which is a provincial norm. This led to Memphis and Studio Alchymia."[7]

The Radical philosophy had the merit and the immediate effect of enlarging the context of the debate on the problems of industrial design, also involving, to a large degree, social, economic and political aspects. However, as was to be expected, its provoking ambiguities caused strong reactions from the old guard. Achille Castiglioni wrote, "Many misunderstandings occured in these last few years during the so-called boom of Italian design, but I think that in Italy the best examples of design have been realized in conditions of a clear understanding between the designer, the public and the manufacturer, that is to say between the language of culture and the language of production".[8] And Franco Albini, another designer active since

◄ A view of the 14th Triennale exhibition, held in Milan in 1968. The exhibit shown was called *Young Italy Protests*.

the 1930s, added, "Around 1965, many situations come to an end or a substantial change. The number of architects increases considerably; themes and events acquire political overtones; the values and aims of exhibitions and conventions lose importance and their necessity is no longer felt. The great number (of architects and designers) alienates any dialogue, and although polemics may be sharp, they never become vigorous. Personally, I felt that by now I was free to work independently, outside any current."[9]

Many, such as Scarpa, the brothers Castiglioni, the BBPR team, but also a great number of young designers, transformed their studios into an *insula felix,* isolating themselves from the rest and "continuing to work with constant commitment in a context without coherence" [10] This was made possible with the support from the small- and medium-sized industries, particularly those operating in consumer goods and household articles, that in these years strengthened their ties with the culture of design. The designer ceased to be considered as the exclusive representative of a cultural élite and entered into a more solidly defined professional area.

By then, doubt afflicted even the most renowned names. The 14th Triennale would be remembered as the *Triennale della contestazione* (The Triennale of dissent). One of its themes was "Great Numbers," referring to mass production, and it also tackled the so far little-known topic of ecology. But the events of May 1968 overthrew everything. The year 1968 marked the end of an era. In that year, in all industrialized countries, a whole generation of young people stood up to declare that they could not possibly identify themselves with the materialistic, consumption-oriented way of life that, so far, had distinguished their epoch. At the cost of considerable hardships, they tried through new sociological and technological experiences to find a different social order. For design, the answer seemed to be in contributing to the resolution of community problems.

In spite of everything, the decade ended with a satisfactory balance. Vittorio Gregotti defined Italian design as, "formally very successful and capable of bridging, with brilliant aesthetic solutions, the gaps in a production system which still has to develop all its possibilities to satisfy the potential market demand and still has to reach maturity in technology and organization, often characterized by improvised methods."[11]

Notes

[1] *La sedia in materia plastica,* Milano: Centrokappa, 1975; *The Museum of Modern Art, New York,* New York: Abrams, 1984

[2] Alberto Rosselli, "Commiato", *Stile Industria,* n.41, February 1963

[3] Giulio Carlo Argan, speech at the 17° Convegno internazionale di artisti/critici/studiosi d'arte, Rimini: 1968

[4] Sergio Asti, speech at the 17° Convegno internazionale di artisti/critici/studiosi d'arte, Rimini, 1968

[5] Superstudio, "Design d'invenzione e di evasione", *Domus,* n.475, June 1969

[6] "It is called Valentine and was invented for use in any place except in an office, so as not to remind anyone of monotonous working hours, but rather to keep amateur poets company on quiet Sundays in the country or to provide a highly colored object on a table in a studio apartment." *Abitare,* n.77 July/August, 1969 "Charlie Townsend, from Cardiff, man of letters, takes *Valentina* with him on weekends and sits and types on the grass." Text in advertisements and posters for the *Valentina* by Ettore Sottsass, Jr. and Roberto Pieraccini, written by Giovanni Giudici and Luigi Fruttero.

[7] Peter Buchanan, "E fu subito stile," *Class,* November 1987

[8] Achille Castiglioni, *Milano 70/70,* Milano: Poldi Pezzoli, p.165

[9] Franco Albini, *Milano 70/70,* p.43

[10] Franco Albini, *Milano 70/70,* p.44

[11] Vittorio Gregotti, *Orizzonti nuovi dell'architettura italiana,* Milano: Electa, 1969

The 1970s

Between 1969 and 1971, Italy passed through a period characterized by violent political unrest and strikes and by a sharp decline in productivity that, followed by the oil crisis of 1973, culminated in 1975 with the strongest economic depression since World War II. It was a very difficult period for Italian design; its role became eroded by the tightening purse strings of the industrial client, put to the test by the economic crisis. The years of the economic miracle were passed, and the productive pause caused by the crisis allowed a chance for reexamination of the past experiences and new stylistic investigations. Italian design entered into a period of reflection, stimulated also by a doctrinal crisis. The professional deadlock, a consequence of a period in which very few new objects came to be produced, added up to the collapse of the modernist dogma.

Above all, ideas were missing, and many proposals of these latter years, in attempting at all costs to be futuristic, no longer represented creative solutions, but improvised and modest contrivances. Some alleged new forces were no more than oddities that quickly wore themselves out because they had nothing to say, even as restyling. The designer tried in vain to recover lost ground, trying to have a say in the different phases of the product designed by him. He loudly demonstrated his own unrealistic intention to assume control of the whole production cycle, from the design phase, through the distribution, right up to the consumption by the final user. He tried to take on tasks which institutionally did not concern him, and that no one was ready to bestow upon him. He pretended in practice to become, and to substitute for, the technical office, the manufacturer, the advertising agent and the sociologist.

This period was characterized by the splitting of Italian designers into two opposing camps. Borrowing a definition from Umberto Eco, they can be identified as "Apocalypsed" and "Integrated". The first group completely identified with the post-1968 revolution. They suffered a deep crisis of values, considering themselves as the creative part of that phenomenon of industrial production and related the drive to consumption that, from Marcuse onwards, came to be identified for a whole decade as the source of all the evils of humanity. Thus, they demonstrated their dissent, refusing any work which could have been considered an aid to capitalism. The more intransigent of them radicalized certain forms of ready-made design, or delved into design for the underdeveloped countries. The moderates, influenced by theories such as those of Victor Papanek (his book *Design for the Real World,* first published in 1970, had a widespread effect as a university text), dedicated themselves to design with utopian finality, for mostly social purposes and for an exclusively public clientele, as a reaction against the industries which oriented their production only for a well-to-do minority. The "integrated" tended in turn to radicalize their position of insertion in the productive mechanism by means of a super-specialization directed toward engineering. In fact, the foundation of structures such as Italdesign and the ever-tightening collaboration between professionals like Renzo Piano with Fiat, or Mario Bellini with Renault, date back to this period. As happened towards the end of the 1960s, and as it has continued to be for the best part of the 1980s, the "culture of the factory" ran parallel to, and surveyed with mixed sentiments of contempt and admiration, the rapid convulsion of high culture.

The principal characteristic of design in the 1970s was, above all, the constitution of a double line of design activity (in some cases almost a double soul existed in a single person). On the one hand, design tried to intensify (and to extend to big industry) the traditional activity linked to the world of production with a growing specialization. This was accompanied by a crisis of values and a fall of

▼ The Tizio lamp was developed by Richard Sapper for Artemide in 1970. It is one of the best-selling lamps in history and has become a symbol of Italian design excellence.

that ideal tension that went beyond just satisfying the individual creativity; the designer questioned his real social usefulness. On the other hand, Italian designers discovered a world of poetic license, in constant and involved contact with the world of the visual arts, and of fashion, always up-to-date with the rapid changes of social taste.

In the 1970s, the success of Italian design, that in the 1960s asserted itself on the internal market, became truly international. It was in this uniquely creative period that many milestones were designed, such as the *Tizio* lamp, designed in 1972 by Richard Sapper (15,000 *Tizio* were sold in 1986 in the USA alone), or the 1974 *VW Golf,* by Giorgio Giugiaro, that, because of their popularity and excellence, have entered the realm of the classic. An uncontrolled production was unleashed, in which all were involved, and by which all were dazzled.

Internationally, it was then considered ''chic'' and ''in'' to be surrounded by Italian products, and ''Italian'' design became synonymous with ''beautiful'' design. Never before had the sector of design represented the defects and virtues of the Italian people, with those self-same excesses of genius and intemperance mixed with scarce morals and great bursts of ideals, that consolidated the image people abroad have, and that the Italian designer would deny, considering it banal or stereotypical. De Pas, D'Urbino, Lomazzi commented, ''Of course, since in these years there has been the new Italian domestic landscape, the Italian look and the Italian line, etc., it is hard to understand very well if one thing is meant or another, because everything in the magazines and in the exhibitions goes together, and each one of us can become a fashionable designer, and abroad (even if we don't count much in architecture and urban planning, and it damn well irritates us, so much so that we are always talking about these things in schools and at congresses) anything goes:

► Combining German technology with Italian flair, the Golf, manufactured by Volkswagen, is a 1974 Giorgio Giugiaro design.

the Italians and the Italian taste and the Mediterranean fantasy and the Italian genius and disorderliness, and so on in a *Zeffirellian* fashion. The only thing still missing is someone like Christo that wraps up with spaghetti the Museum of Modern Art in New York, which in May exhibits all the stuff mentioned above, and the picture is complete."[1]

In spite of the crisis, the field of furniture, particularly in the area of home furnishings, continued to introduce interesting products. Vico Magistretti, Gae Aulenti, the ever-present Castiglionis, and others, created, with brilliant quality of invention, with the elegance of aesthetic solutions, a truly new culture of design for the home which, even with different answers and values, would remain in the future the most complete and significant fact of Italian design in the 1970s.

The theme of the design of office space, on the other hand, roused little interest. In fact, in this climate of general protest, the Italian designer could not free himself from feelings of guilt provoked by the continuous accusations of being subservient to the ruling classes. Furthermore, he was caught off balance by new trends brought in by the United States in "open-plan" furnishings, and the resulting formal revolution that, having been started by the Americans, remains their almost exclusive domain for product and project quality.

Italians began, nevertheless, especially in working tools and machines for the office, to take human engineering and ergonomics into account, analyzing the relationships that exist between man and the reality with which he comes into contact. The study of proportions that objects must have, with consequential study of anatomy and the theory of perception and psycho-physiology of work, carried an important weight in the modification of the production phases and methods.

Going over the acts of the various conferences, debates, lectures and exhibition catalogues of this period, it seems that, as a response to a quite confused demand for a greater adherence to reality, there was a far-from-concrete debate. Echoes of 1968, mixed with the claim of the social responsibility of design, were expressed in essentially political terms. Utopia and political provocation became the two extremes with which the flashy side of design tended to show itself, in the end alienating itself. Between the two extremes, there seemed to be a kind of no-man's land, about which the intellectuals did not deign to show interest.

In 1972, the exhibition, *Italy—The New Domestic Landscape* opened in New York, curated by Emilio Ambasz and promoted by the Museum of Modern Art. Two clearly distinct sections were presented. A historical review of 160 objects for the home, considered among the most significant of all the products in Italy in the preceding decade, was shown, along with suggested homes of the future. The invited designers were asked to design spaces and objects that characterized domestic life, proposing "micro-environments and micro-events". The critic Bruno Zevi observed the occasion as the abandoning of the binomial "from the spoon to the city" proclaimed by Rogers; the Italian designer seemed inclined to be satisfied with the spoon, taking shelter in the "almost incommunicable isolation of the domestic myth." Generally, the exhibition was seen as an expression of art and Utopia, more than of design. No one was prepared to believe that such "sensations" could influence the realities of production and sales. Yet the exhibition was important to the acceptance of the unusual and the excessive.

The exhibition also highlighted a phenomenon that became widespread during the period in question. The "paper project" that has no contact with the production reality, whose exclusive clients are galleries and museums, was embraced. As had already occurred in the past, when the possibilities of concrete outlets became rare and ideas uncertain, the drawing emerged again, filling the role of romantic refuge and allowing expression of a repressed creativity.

In the era of the economic miracle, time was too short and one had to work very quickly, because the factory and the market would not wait. Drawings were essentially technical and all that went beyond constructive details was considered an affectation, a superfluous preciousness. Belonging to the same epoch were various short-lived experiences that fell under the influence of the American avant-garde, and of oriental religious thought. In this cultural context, the anti-industrial ideological positions developed, associated with the idea of a return to the land and agriculture and a general anti-consumption polemic. These theories, supported primarily by the younger generations, brought about contradictory experiences, such as that of *poor design, (design povero),* that, in the first half of the 1970s, fought for the revival of the traditional craftsmanship with "natural" techniques and materials derived from a peasant culture, by then largely gone, even in Italy. Standing out in this trend, though with different orientations, were Andrea Branzi, Riccardo Dalisi and Ettore Sottsass, Jr.

The global problems that emerged between 1968 and the energy crisis and its economic backlashes imposed a rethinking of the philosophy of Italian design and the way it had developed in the two preceding decades. Many young designers refused the slightly aristocratic attitude of their predecessors, who were by then famous. They protested against the structure of the big exhibitions, beginning with the Triennale, and of prizes, such as the Compasso d'Oro.

The deep crisis that shook Italian design was revealed even by the furious battle for power which erupted within the Association for Industrial Design (ADI). A report presented to the Meeting of July 10, 1973 gives a good idea of the ideological climate of the moment: "ADI, as an institution, in the bounds of the general crisis of all the social structures, has reached its level of incompetence; a condition of crisis from which appear new events and forces . . . It is useless to try and give a congruous and united image of the association to the outside, inasmuch as the divergences within ADI are as explosive as in society without. Development and underdevelopment are both structured to the system. Opulence and restricted circumstances blend easily within ADI, along with designer-manager directed firms with middle industry turnovers; meanwhile, there are members that have incomes comparable to public assistance."

The ultimate objective of some of the protesters was to transform the association into a union. Paradoxically, the maneuver failed because of the open diffidence of the central trade union, that could not understand how this category of professionals related to the working class. The crisis with which ADI was battling mirrored that of other institutions connected with design. The Triennale, after the occupation of 1968, tried to reopen two years later than the regular deadline, but even this 15th edition was deserted by Italian architects and designers. The reasons were mostly political and were summarized in a note from ADI which called upon the Triennale to, "receive the line of socializing the design and cultural work and to face wide-ranging themes matured by the struggles undertaken by the democratic forces of the country". A certain mode of expression was typical of these years, in which every aspect of private life became politicized, and demagogy and populism reached a paroxysm in Italy. De Pas, D'Urbino, Lomazzi wrote at the time, "Good intentions par excellence, those that ennoble us and with which we adorn ourselves, like everyone in the meetings between colleagues and at every other important occasion, couldn't be missing, and in fact, are not—the socio-political intentions—but it is too difficult to talk about these because in the end we should say it with the drawing. There is certainly the desire to summarize them in the definition of democratic design."[2]

While ADI and the Triennale discussed and battled for their refoundation, the Compasso d'Oro also came under harsh attack, accused of taking an almost exclusive interest in the formal aspects of products, of ignoring both the social and technological aspects of design, reducing it to one of the many branches of the figurative arts. Furthermore, many designers refused to restrict their professional commitment solely to the designing of objects, and sustained the necessity instead of a greater contribution to environmental design (work ambience, decoration of urban space, sign systems).

Designers discovered themselves as philosophers. Their discussions concerned the contradictions and the compromises that the intellectual is forced to accept in a capitalist society. Environments were searched for in which the designer could operate to succeed in the twofold operation of "unmasking" the ambiguities of society, designing in such a way that an object destined for production would not lose its own disruptive charge.

The Compasso d'Oro organizers tried to face the critics, deepening the relationships with fields different from those traditionally covered by the prize, in particular those tied to the resolving of the problems of the collectivity and to a new use of the city. For these reasons, in comparison to previous editions, the 13th Compasso d'Oro in 1970 was decisively focused on the theme of public

services, taking an interest, among many others, in the design of sanitary and scholastic services and of collective transportion, sectors in which Italy was notably behind in comparison to other countries. Since the industries were still reticent to finance research in this field, one of the ambitious objectives of the prize was to provide the public bodies with stimuli and indications that allowed them to become, from simple buyers, leading characters in the process of the design and realization of social services.

In spite of the new openings, the Compasso d'Oro was suspended, and only in 1977 were there positive moves to resume it. As a first move, the Region of Lombardy sponsored a review of Italian design in the 1950s in which its organizers expressed their intention to recover a "heritage of ideas and stimuli for the most part lost". As it turned out, they needed two more years to finally produce a new edition of the Compasso d'Oro prize. In effect, the grave shortages in the sector of equipment for collective use (as well as the economic difficulties of more traditional fields) pushed many designers to address their design intervention in this direction. The experience was completely new. In fact, the destination of use of the objects, individual or collective, modified profoundly the methodology of designing, and in this case it was necessary to underline certain aspects, such as security and trustworthiness, which were previously underestimated.

A few bold initiatives in the field of design of products for collective use date back to the 1970s. Particularly interesting is the program carried out by ATM, the public transportation authority of Milan, that renewed all its means of transportation (tram, bus, subway), including the interiors. The confusion and the loss of direction from the traditional institutes, from the Triennale to the Compasso d'Oro, gave a growing importance to the Milan Furniture Fair, as a primary source of information on new trends for

▼ The Boby, designed in 1970 by Joe Colombo, is a drafting/art supply cart. Manufactured by Bieffeplast, it is made of ABS plastic.

designers, architects, dealers and the producers themselves.

In 1977, the publication of a new magazine dedicated to design, *Modo,* bogan performing, as stated in its first issue, "an act of faith even in difficult moments in history such as this".[3] The new review joined the many which already existed at the time, and with these shared a market of small but steady dimensions, with about twenty-five thousand readers.

In the years from 1976–79, there was a gradual abatement of social unrest, a progressive overcoming of the so-called *Lead years* that had seen the culmination of political terrorism and a strong productive resurgence. This was triggered off by the vitality and capacity for improvisation of the small and medium industries and of the increased activity of the so-called underground economy (a magma formed by small craftsmen and workshops that maintained, in addition to their official activity, one or more "moonlighting" operations). This coincided with a revival of interests in the industry of design. Very little remained of the revolutionary ideals of ten years before.

Notes

[1] J. De Pas, D. D'Urbino, P. Lomazzi, "I nostri buoni propositi", *Milano 70/70,* Milano: Museo Poldi Pezzoli, vol.3, p.166

[2] Ibid, p.166

[3] Alessandro Mendini, "Design dove vai", *Modo,* n.1, June 1977, p.13

The 1980s: New Opportunities

In the past decade, there has been such a frenzied succession of the most varying cultural trends that it has been difficult to find one's orientation without confusion or deviation. Experiments have often been exhausted before completion. Understanding their nature and value has been hindered by the abstractness to which they are confined, as they often fail to pass from theoretical enunciation to practical realization. Due to its scarce adherence to concrete problems and because of the ephemeral nature of its products, this fast evolution—which runs parallel to the development of customs and technology—implies the constant risk of degrading to a mere fashion phenomenon. However, in spite of its often severe limits, this phenomenon has the merit of evidencing problems and anxieties which would be absurd to ignore.

In a profession where survival has always required a considerable flair in knowing how to take advantage of public relations, self-promotion strongly depends on provocation. Considered indispensable, provocation has been regimented and reduced to a rigid norm that seems to have become design's main objective. In Italy, the most conspicuous part of today's design seems, above all, characterized by a kind of well-aimed exhibitionism, by calculated folly, expressed by designers who claim to be the prophets of avant-garde ideas and who, at the same time, exploit a glorious tradition. There is only one basic idea, to stun with an image, however unpleasant or contrary to common sense and good taste. It may be a poor idea, but if it's clad in loud attire it garners attention. From a cultural point of view, this creates great confusion and a stagnation of ideas. The confusion also involves the clientele. The industry of furniture and objects for the home, which maintains close and important ties with design, has lately based its production more on image than on precise marketing strategies. The object based on design, all the better if it is eccentric, is supposed to make up for the lack of marketing and distribution analysis.

Yet, innovation does not necessarily have to pass through provocation, especially if a design has nothing new to propose, and, if from an element of rupture, it has become a fad. The bait thrown to the critics has, little by little, become a gesture of reverence and eventually servile submission by designers who have abdicated from their role as creators. The creative function has been taken over by the critic, who, through the specialized press, now dictates the new choices and trends.

Toward the end of the 1970s, Milan's post-radical avant-garde emerged, more or less headed by Ettore Sottsass, Alessandro Mendini and Andrea Branzi. The Alchymia and Memphis groups (operations cleverly piloted and financed by companies who had been committed for years to the production of a much more traditional design), were the first to attempt a revolution.

"Founded in 1976 as a graphic studio and after a rather hazy start as sponsor of radical, sometimes poor projects, Alchymia was to become in 1978, and stay for another two years, the depository of the most important research and projects."[1] With regard to Memphis, the choice of its name was purely casual. The story goes that one night the founders grouped around their guru Sottsass. After having emptied a considerable number of bottles, they decided to name their experiment after the Bob Dylan song that was being played at the moment. To divert from the rich classic elegance of the then well-established tradition of Italian design, Memphis and Alchymia committed themselves to creating objects of perversely antifunctional bad taste.

Memphis proposed a style based on a provocative figurative language tending to give priority to the spectacular element, or the image over functionality. The output

◄ The Wink, a folding armchair/lounge
chair, was designed in 1980 by Toshiyuki
Kita for Cassina.

was characterized by cheap materials, loud colors and surface decoration, renunciation of industrial production (since
this would anyway be impossible) and shocking prices.
The production was planned to transform what the traditional designer used to consider as a fault, such as small
number and short life, into a merit for a very restricted
market, consisting mainly of collectors. In fact, despite its
extraordinary success in the press, the survival of Memphis could only be guaranteed by the high cost of furniture, while that of Alchymia can be ensured only by exhibition and publicity.

The object is no longer the product of a professional
ambition to improve something that has so far been made
poorly and fails to please, or create something that is still
missing. Form prevails over functionality and sometimes
reveals its constructive pretext only after thorough examination. The geometric forms are not always primary and
elementary, and only their arrangement recomposes
images already visualized in the mind.

The lack of balance of these volumetric composi-
tions plays on the equivocal effect of accurately avoided
centers of gravity, to emphasize the form's absurd equilib-
rium. The results are freakish lamps, libraries with oblique
running shelves creating a sculptural effect. Briefly, the
structures tremble and are crystallized in a mobility that
has nothing to do with the futuristic concept of represent-
ing movement, but only conveys a sensation of nervous-
ness. Interiors become one big comic strip, governed only
by imagination.

The object in the 1980s is loaded with semantic
characteristics that don't belong to it, and so chairs are
created that don't look like chairs, multi-use tables that can
hardly be used as tables. They are chameleon-like objects
with manifold purposes, some of which are rather vague.
Objects that must be clever, amusing, kitschy, high-brow

or complicated, that boil down to much ado about nothing
and soon show their age are the norm. Here, the colors go
beyond the rules of vision—acid hues are matched with
bright ones. "Before Memphis, color in furniture didn't
exist" Barbara Radice stated. The result of these
choices—which certainly had never been used in élite
design—finds adhesion elsewhere, in spontaneous and
casual solutions reminiscent of motels and suburbs. The
palimpsest of colors is, however, well ordered; to each of
the product's elements a certain color scheme corre-
sponds, as if to make it stand out quite clearly. Colored
surfaces alternate with linear, rigorously black and white
ones, elementary graffiti that would make Gottfried Sem-
per, the father of geometrism, shiver. Lacquered wood is
contrasted with embossed laminates, in an irreverent
shiny/opaque patchwork. Commas running amok crowd
Sottsass's *Bacteria* laminate pattern and immediately
infest all fashionable interiors.

Thanks to wide and hammering publicity, and to the
constant revival of every artistic phenomenon, even the
most horrible creations have the chance to become utterly
chic. Bad taste and uselessness having the advantage of
being within everybody's reach, many minor designers
from Spain to California find, through emulation, the opportunity of sharing the limelight.

The range of these trends is limited to furniture and
interior decoration and rarely goes beyond the phase of
prototypes. A "new handicraft industry" is flourishing,
where the production is limited to small series of more or
less experimental works. The production of pieces not
strictly tied to commercial logic (figurative typologies that
transcend the traditional schemes) may represent a strong
point, as the expression of ongoing innovative research, or
may indicate a congenital weakness that implies giving
priority to vague poetic research, rather than intelligently

I Feltri, a seating collection designed by Gaetano Pesce, was introduced by Cassina in 1987. Constructed of thick felt, the chairs' lower portions are impregnated with thick resin, while the upper portion of each chair can be folded down or left upright.

facing the problems connected with commercial production.

Of course, the individual piece may also influence mass production, but in the case of these recent phenomena, their construction implies abandoning industrial culture for a product that is justifiable only through the dictates of fashion. The inevitable result is a growing discrepancy between market and project. Great creativity is sometimes stifled by a lack of solid professionality. Many of the most famous designers who have emerged in the last few years have no specific knowledge of materials or technologies. Therefore, the contrast gets sharper between the two different visions, of those who produce for the market and of those "who work for culture, writing about things, producing events, happenings and topics for debates."[2]

The so-called new culture of design in the 1970s, which tended toward an often provocative linguistic re-elaboration, has helped to give designing a role of mediation between the heterogeneous culture of consumption and the pragmatic one of manufacturing. The trouble is that the latest avant-garde movements have tried to limit communication of the object to mere communication, doing their best to ignore the question of its production and thus confining themselves to projects that will never go beyond the drafting phase or the prototype.

Looking back at what has been done over the past twenty years, it is not difficult to see that the architectural battles of the so-called Radicals represented only one evident but marginal factor of the vast transformations that concerned all aspects of the industrial society. This structural passage involved manufacturing processes, technology, market organization and, consequently, the languages and methods of designing. Industry has faced, and largely accepted, a growing culturalization of products, realizing the importance of a good company image. Yet, merely creating an image has proved inadequate in facing the problems of present-day design. The times of useless experiments for the sake of experiment are gone; designing requires a solid cultural background and technical insight, the market requires constant high quality and specialization.

Outside the furniture branch, the impact of the new avant-garde is very scarce. Follies à la Memphis have no chance when it comes to designing cars or refrigerators that have to work. As Mario Bellini put it, "There are no postmodern cars. Fiat makes cars that are banal, but you can use them."[3] However, from the beginning of the 1980s, even in those branches of industry where innovation is slower and more lengthily pondered, there is also a change in the design philosophy. The final product is no longer considered as something definite that will be manufactured without variants and in huge quantities destined for an undifferentiated public. So far, the illusion of mass production had been based on the idea of creating a democratic product that would answer all the market's requirements, with the very fact of being mass-produced sufficient evidence of the product's good quality. The manufacturers feel that there are different markets and that only a high degree of flexibility will make it possible to appeal to the different tastes of the various consumer groups.

Industrial automation enables a company to produce different versions, almost with a personalized touch, of one and the same model, starting from an identical basic structure and enriching it with options. Unfortunately, inadequate theoretical knowledge and technical weakness often leave the designer unprepared for coping with the new requirements. If some designers of the older generation do not keep in step with the times, the situation

▶ Marco Zanini's Dublin sofa was introduced as part of the 1981 Memphis Collection, which challenged the established ideals of good taste in furniture design.

seems to be worse for the exponents of *New Design,* who have often shown an inability to connect an idea with a good functional product. They seek refuge in handicraft, in works to be realized in small series, in the grand artistic gesture, thus abandoning all the premises and objectives that form the base of industrial design.

In the 1980s, Italian designers pursue, with different degrees of conviction and comprehensiveness, varied theoretical and political positions. The Italian design style presents different "veins". Its range is from linear and rigorous functionalism to "real design" which gives in to the slightest change in taste. From models by fashion designers, searching for elegance and refinement, to the hard plasticity of technological design and from the "ecological" trend to the neo-avant-garde, radical postmodern, Italian design has kept its vitality and, after a period of deeply felt crisis, is again consolidating its image as a creative, fanciful, expressive tool, able to surprise year after year with formal innovations. It offers unexpected effects in a blend of research, play, advanced technology and ironic adventures; and creates objects that are acceptable to the market and, at the same time, able to provoke debate and stimulate different visions. The elaborate theories of the previous years have been translated into often banal products that are miles away from the pursued result. What is left of these theories is the desire for a strong formal idea with sculptural features.

The intellectual climate reflects the renewed tendency to keep both feet on the ground. Many members of the younger generation have realized that design had gradually drifted away from everyday reality and neglected the problems of technology and manufacturing. The designers have rediscovered the need for a more pragmatic approach to these problems and the importance of making designs that, no longer conditioned by any ideological manifesto,

aim for the creation of a product not geared to the whims of cultural fashion.

It is obvious that design cannot be reduced to its mere relationship with the industry and the commercial distribution of the products, but it is just as clear that research and experimentation cannot do without the production system. Facing real and concrete, even prosaic questions requires realism and objectivity.

One of the strong points of Italian design that has been recovered is the synergy between manufacturer and designer. This results in tightened relationships between design, technological research, industrial production, communication of the product via advertising, and new markets. "The designer can no longer afford to see himself as an artistic project operator, because he risks becoming bizarre and there is no sharp line drawn between the bizarre and the ridiculous. The designer avails himself of the same cultural and physical instruments of the manufacturer in order to be able to discuss things on equal terms."[4]

Notes

[1] Barbara Radice, *Memphis,* New York: Rizzoli, 1984
[2] Michele De Lucchi, interview, *Modo,* n.98, April–May 1987
[3] *Modo,* n.71–72, August-September 1984
[4] Angelo Cortesi at the ADI meeting of March 3, 1987

The Production

Introduction

Italian design is an indiscriminate term, given the many ways in which creativity is expressed in Italy. The sector in question is teeming with initiative, overflowing with the most diverse outcomes, involved in the most discordant directions: human, social, economic, technical, etc. As a consequence, its definitions have varied with extraordinary volubility in relation to the changing valuations that the militant critics have placed on it, with minimal change to the substance of the actual designs.

The picture that we will attempt to trace could seem, therefore, somewhat unfocused, but this lack of focus is, in part, a reflection of the Italian design scene, with its innumerable themes and interests and as many techniques, orientated in the most heterogeneous and divergent, sometimes even opposite, directions. It is inevitable that, considering the limited space available, some objects of high quality will be left out. Without pursuing the illusion of completeness, only objects currently in production will be included, limiting the choice of the historic objects to those products that have contributed to a great extent to the definition of the image of Italian design. The qualities (both aesthetic and functional) and the historic significance (innovative capacity) of each object have been considered. Obviously, these are mostly subjective criteria that mirror the authors' own logic and perspective. The choice of an object according to its historic importance could lead to the selection of an unconvincing object from an aesthetic or functional point of view, but its contribution to the advancement of design might be too important to be ignored. An object is chosen for its ability to embody, or for having helped to create, those ideals of aesthetic perfection that have become an integral part of our epoch; objects that are evocative of sensations, expressions or ways to communicate a style of life.

The Italian eclecticism, the absence of a style or of

a single ideology, results in a perhaps excessive number of directions, surprising in comparison with other countries, especially those of northern Europe where a certain stylistic immutability is characteristic. While it is important to communicate the variety of such aspects, for their innovative and experimental characteristics, and for their lively contribution to the diffusion of the image of Italian design at an international level, the authors have chosen to exclude ephemeral styles or those of questionable influence, aside from their extensive but short-lived press coverage. While only objects actually put into production have been taken into consideration, leaving out the unrealized projects, of which every designer has drawersfull, it has nevertheless been decided to include some objects whose production is only partially industrialized, or produced in relatively limited series (as for example, the Ferrari automobiles), because of their important contributions in the determination of the dominant machine aesthetic.

This part of the book is meant to give a broader view of Italian design, ranging from structural elements and building materials to cars and boats, even airplanes, cameras and leisure products. It has been decided to exclude fashion products, bound essentially to factors of style and taste, and thus generally ephemeral. Weapons, on the other hand, have been included, as they are undoubtedly among the most highly designed and fascinating objects of human production. We disagree with those, and there are many among critics and museum curators, who have decided to simply ignore them. It would seem limiting and intolerant to express a moral judgement about an object and decide to ignore it based on its potential use in anti-social activities.

Included among the Italian designers are a certain number of non-Italian names. Rather than focusing on the geographic origin or registered citizenship of the creator,

the cultural formation and design experiences have been taken into account for cases in which the results are typically Italian, or reflective of Italian-based design philosophies.

As a result of the absence of specialist archives, and, in many cases, the destruction or dispersion of the actual objects, the consultation of documentation and sources, or the finding of photographs, drawings and sketches, dating back to just a few years ago, is therefore very difficult. The only easily accessible sources, magazines and catalogues, are generally incomplete and imprecise, often leaving one in doubt as to whether a certain object was actually mass-produced or whether it remained only at the prototype stage. In a country where the problem of the conservation of an immense heritage of pictorial and sculptural, architectural and monumental masterpieces that have emerged from every historical epoch seems unsolvable, the safeguard of recent industrial products becomes practically impossible to propose.

It is not the intention nor the ambition of this book to draw a balance of the work produced by the latest generations of Italian designers, nor to represent a manifesto of a new trend. Drawing the balance would require objectivity and complete information. Issuing a manifesto cannot be done without clear, unilateral ideas and a strong polemic attitude—all factors that are lacking. Today it is, in any case, difficult to become sufficiently detached to judge the latest propositions in the field of design. The fast evolution in consumption does not allow any idea to take root. Stylistic nostalgia, revivals, new academies, science fiction, styling and spontaneous design have all found expression in a vast production almost immediately outdated, with only a few classic exceptions.

TRANSPORTATION

■ The Cagiva T4 350E cross-country motorcycle, designed in 1987, has a single-cylinder, four-stroke engine, electronic ignition and a top speed of 145 km/h.

▼ Originally designed in 1946 by Corradino d'Ascanio for Piaggio, the Vespa PX model motorbike has a single-cylinder, two-stroke engine, electronic ignition and a top speed of 110 km/h.

■ The Gilera GSA 50 moped was designed in 1985. It has a single-cylinder, two-stroke engine and electric starting system.

■ The Quasar Tender is a collapsible
▼ moped, introduced in 1984 and
designed by Italo Cammarata. The
moped weighs only 15 kg and can
be easily carried.

■ The Bicimosquito, designed in
1946 by Garelli, is an auxilliary
engine for bicycles, here shown on
a woman's model. Turning any
bicycle into a moped able to reach
speeds of 30 km/hr, the engine
can easily be disengaged when
conventional bicycle riding is pre-
ferred.

■ The ETR 450 Pendolino, designed
in 1985–88 by the engineers of
Fiat Ferroviaria, is an electric train
with tilting body mechanism that
permits higher speed travel around
curves.

■ The Jumbotram, designed by
▼ Giovanni Klaus Koenig and Roberto
Segoni in collaboration with the
Milan Transit Authority, is
manufactured by Fiat.

■ The Spazio bus was designed for Iveco in 1977 by Isao Hosoe and Antonio Barrese.

▼ Giorgio Giugiaro designed the Volvo Italia 99 long-distance bus in 1983.

■ The Spazio bus has a higher back roof line to relieve the claustrophobic effect of the 11-meter long interior space.

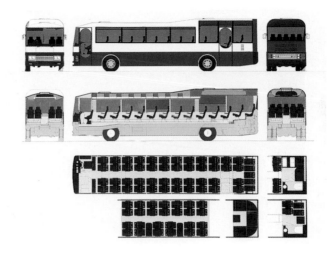

■ Bruno Giardino's design for a covered chairlift unit is made of reinforced fiberglass and was first produced in 1986 by Leitner.

■ Aerial tramway car, designed by Bruno Giardino in 1985, accommodates 12 passengers. It has a steel frame, covered by a reinforced fiberglass shell. Manufacturer: Leitner.

■ Egidio Sculati's Baglietto 46-meter yacht, with a top speed of 25 knots, was designed in 1986.

▼ Designed in 1983, the Black Corsair Grand Soleil yacht, a 60-foot racing model with a top speed of 39 knots, is manufactured by Riva.

■ Riva's 1960 Aquarama Special, a
▼ sleek "runabout" with fine mahogany detailing, is 8.75 meters long and offers a top speed of 82 km/h.

■ The C22J/Caproni Vizzola two-seater jet, designed in 1987 for military or commercial use, has a lenticular fuselage that increases the aircraft's aerodynamics.

▼ The Avanti P180, a turbo-prop plane marketed to corporations, was designed in 1987.

■ A twin-turbine helicopter designed in 1975, the A109 Medevac can transport eight passengers at a top speed of 300 km/h.

▼ Introduced in 1976, the A21S glider, designed by Carlo Ferrarin and Livio Sonzio, can accommodate two passengers. A microjet engine provides power.

■ The Ferrari Testarossa, designed
▼ by Battista Pininfarina in 1984,
shown with and without rear
spoiler, is a luxurious sports car
inside with a sleek, aerodynamic
exterior.

■ An interior view of the Testarossa,
with its luxurious appointments,
such as contoured leather
upholstery.

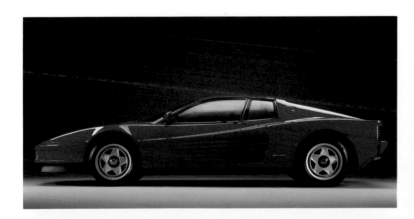

■ The 1980 Fiat Panda model, designed by Giorgio Giugiaro, brought a more aerodynamic shape to the company's compact car line, which was characterized during the 1970s by more boxy-shaped models.

■ The Aurelia Spider B24 was designed by the Pininfarina firm in 1950. The first model, manufactured by Lancia, was introduced in 1955.

▼ The 1983 Fiat Uno, designed by Giorgio Giugiaro, was deemed "Car of the Year" in 1984. It is the best-selling car of the Fiat line. The compact car's top speed is 155 km/h.

■ Battista Pininfarina's Alfa Romeo Spider Duetto was designed in 1966.

▼ The 1980 Furgonetta Panda, an adaptation of the Giorgio Giugiaro Fiat sedan model, is a mini-van, with extended rear compartment for increased storage capability.

■ The Delta, a 1979 Lancia model designed by Giorgio Giugiaro, was voted "Car of the Year" in 1980 and maintains a high-performance reputation among racing car enthusiasts.

▼ Nuccio Bertone's Miura, a 12-cylinder, mid-engine, two-seat sports car, was designed in 1965 for Lamborghini.

RESIDENTIAL
FURNISHINGS

■ The Siglo 20 sofa, designed by Francesco Soro for ICF Italy in 1979, has an enameled, tubular steel frame.

■ Soro's Siglo sofa can be upholstered in leather or fabric. The frame may be left exposed, or can be slipcovered for a more conventional look.

▼ The Strips armchair, designed by Cini Boeri with Laura Griziotti, was introduced by Arflex in 1972. The chair is made from a single block of polyurethane foam.

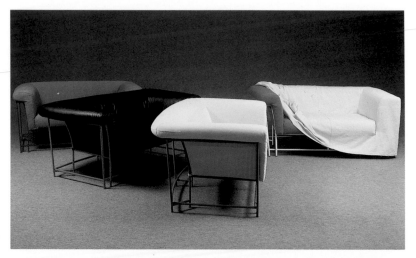

■ The fully adjustable MP40 lounge chair and sofa, designed in 1955 by Osvaldo Borsani for Tecno, can be transformed into beds.

■ The Onda sofa, with tubular stainless-steel frame, was designed in 1985 by De Pas, D'Urbino, Lomazzi for Zanotta.

■ The Diesis sofa was designed in 1979 by Antonio Citterrio and Paolo Nava for B&B Italia.

■ The Sity Collection, produced by
▼ B&B Italia in 1986, offers a range of sectional seating units that can be combined in numerous configurations. The series was designed by Antonio Citterio.

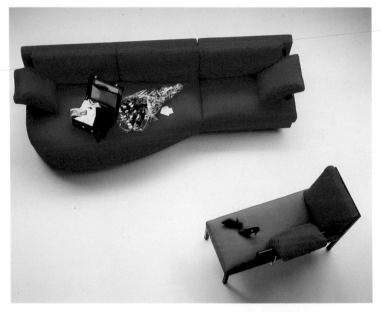

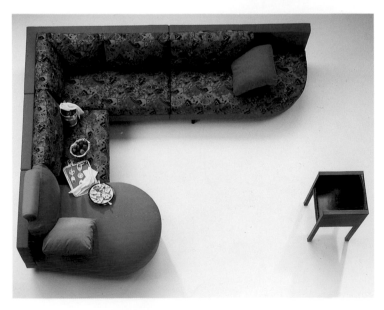

■ Pierluigi Cerri's Ouverture sofa combines the industrial aesthetic of a steel girder-like frame with softly curved upholstery and pillow armrests. The sofa was designed in 1982 and is manufactured by Poltrona Frau.

▼ William Sawaya designed the Editto sofa in 1985 for his own firm, Sawaya & Moroni.

■ The three-seat Veranda sofa was designed by Vico Magistretti in 1984. Produced by Cassina, the sofa's center seating unit is fixed, while the two side units can pivot to create a curved seating unit, with exposed portions of the base serving as built-in table surfaces.

■ The Century, a chaise longue
designed by Andrea Branzi, was
introduced as part of the 1982
Memphis Collection.

■ The Paolina, a chaise longue
designed in 1926, is manufactured
by Poltrona Frau.

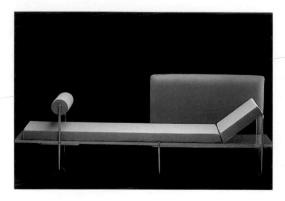

■ Antonio Citterio's Max, a series of curved sofas with distinctive rolled backs, was designed in 1983 for Flexform.

■ The 1982 Phil, also by Citterio, is a sofa manufactured by Flexform.

▼ An update of the classic Tuxedo sofa, the Magister, designed by Antonio Citterio and Paolo Nava, has a perforated metal surface running along the back of the sofa—a contemporary version of the traditional sofa table. Flexform introduced Magister in 1982.

■ The Side 1 and Side 2 chests of drawers were designed by Shiro Kuramata in 1970. Produced by Cappellini International, the dyed ashwood pieces are characterized by their undulating silhouettes.

■ Adolfo Natalini's Volumina secretary was designed in 1987 and is manufactured by Sawaya & Moroni.

▼ The Teco roll-top desk was designed in 1983 by William Sawaya for Sawaya & Moroni.

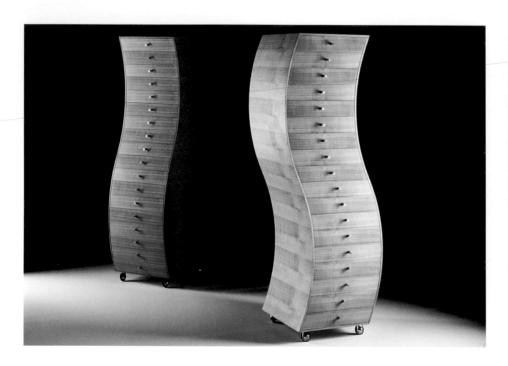

■ Achille Castiglioni's aluminum and wire mesh screen was designed in 1983 and is manufactured by De Padova.

■ The Asseman canopy bed, manufactured by De Padova, was designed in 1983 by Patrizia Cagliani.

▼ Perched atop lacquered metal legs, the dyed-ash Solaris chest of drawers was designed in 1977 by Shiro Kuramata. The piece is manufactured by Cappellini International.

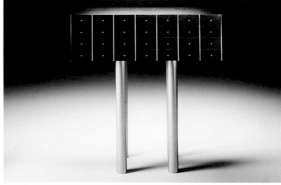

■ The Morgana bed, designed by Paolo Piva in 1987, has a headboard which features built-in side table surfaces. Manufacturer: Poliform.

■ The Teatro bed was designed for Molteni by Luca Meda and Aldo Rossi in 1985.

▼ Luca Meda's Les Beaux Jours chaise longue, in lacquered and natural wood, is as much a piece of sculpture as it is furniture. The austere design was introduced by Molteni in 1986.

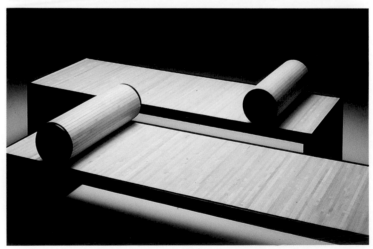

■ The A1, a cabinet designed for the housing of television, video and stereo equipment, was designed in 1987 by the Turri studio. The cabinet doors, covered in leather, slide out to allow full access to the burled maple interior.

■ Vittorio Prato's Flash daybed has a stretched fabric back over a frame of tubular steel. It was designed in 1987 for Interflex.

▼ The Itititi bed was designed in 1985 by Achille Castiglioni and Giancarlo Pozzi for Interflex. The mattress support is provided by a plane of rectangular wood beams.

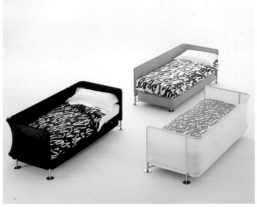

■ Giuseppe Pagano and Gino Levi Montalcini designed the Chichibio, a tubular steel and laminate telephone stand, in 1931. It was reintroduced by Zanotta in 1981.

■ Tubular steel table is part of the Chassis Letto bed system designed in 1980 by Vittorio Prato for Interflex.

■ The Cenacolo table, in black marble, has a metal frame supporting its marble top, giving the impression that the top floats in space. It was designed in 1975 by Giulio Cappellini for Cappellini International.

■ Giotto Stoppino's 4905/6/7 stacking tables were designed in 1968. Manufactured by Kartell, the tables are made of injection-molded ABS plastic.

▼ The Quaderna writing desk, designed in 1970 by Superstudio, is manufactured by Zanotta. The simple wooden desk is covered in a grid-print laminate.

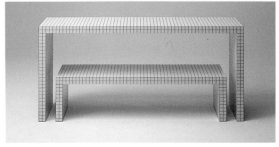

■ The Eros series of marble tables was designed for Skipper in 1971 by Angelo Mangiarotti. Cone-shaped bases interlock with shaped tabletops in a simple, building-block manner to create tables of various sizes.

▼ Silvio Coppola's 612B wooden table was designed in 1970 and is manufactured by Bernini.

■ Anna Castelli Ferrieri designed the 4300 table for Kartell in 1982. It was the first full-height table to be made entirely of injection-molded plastic.

■ The Orio, a metal and glass side table, was designed in 1985 by Pierluigi Cerri and Gregotti Associates for Fontana Arte.

▼ Rectangular Cenacolo marble table was designed in 1975 by Giulio Cappellini.

■ The Pantos table, designed by Bruno Rota in 1984, has a metal base which can be reconfigured to support glass tops of various shapes and sizes. Manufacturer: B & B Italia.

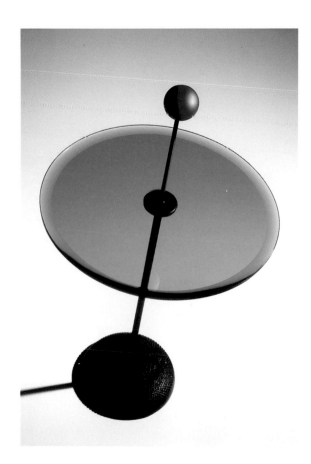

■ The Cumano folding table was designed in 1978 for Zanotta by Achille Castiglioni. Made of enameled steel, the table can be hung from a wall when not in use.

■ Carlo Forcolini's 1984 Apocalypse Now steel table has a built-in light fixture. Manufacturer: Alias.

▼ The 2652 cocktail table, designed by Gae Aulenti in 1980, is a classic high-tech design. Manufacturer: Fontana Arte.

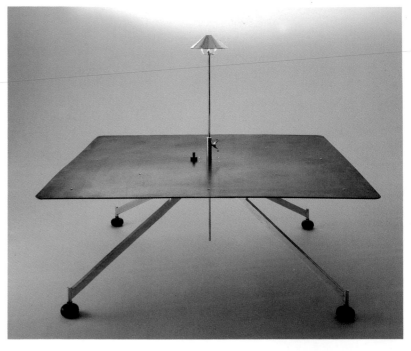

■ The Alanda table system, designed by Paolo Piva in 1982, is based on inverted pyramid-shaped metal structures topped with glass. The tables are manufactured by B&B Italia.

▼ A drafting-table aesthetic is embraced in Toshiyuki Kita's 1983 Alto Basso adjustable table for De Padova.

■ The Tarzan chair and table, designed by Davide Mercatali and Paolo Pedrizzetti for Zeus/Noto in 1985, have "skins" of rubber-like polyurethane over their tubular steel components.

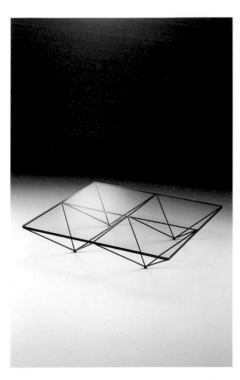

■ Ada Montanari designed the
Positano wool rug in 1987 for Sisal.

■ The Planimetrie, a hand-knotted
wool carpet design by Marco
Zanuso, was first milled in 1987 by
the Sisal Collection.

▼ Bruno Munari's Aloni wool carpet
design of 1987 is produced by
Sisal.

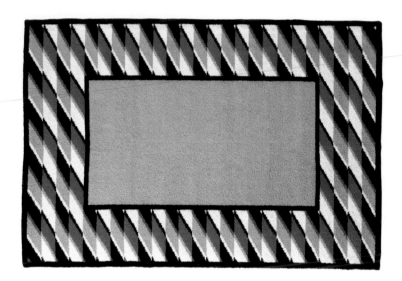

■ Printed cotton sateen fabric, offering a rich sheen, is part of the Strutture line, produced by De Angelis in 1986.

▼ The collection Les Nacres consists of pearlescent printed cotton fabrics designed by the De Angelis firm in 1987.

■ Printed cotton fabric is part of De Angelis' Strutture line of 1986.

▼ Africa Collection of printed cotton fabrics was designed and manufactured by De Angelis in 1985.

■ The Missoni fashion team designed the Mali wool rug in 1987 for the T.J. Vestor firm.

▼ Designed by Vincent Miree for Gaetano Rossini, the Smear pattern of cotton fabrics, introduced in 1987, is achieved through the use of varied textures within a single yard of fabric.

■ The Graffiti collection of cotton textiles offers colorfully bold geometric patterns. The textile collection was introduced in 1987 by Massarelli.

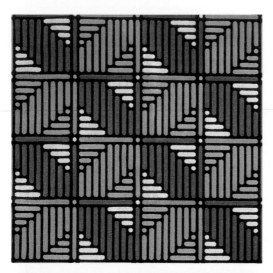

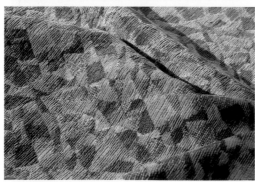

■ The Sequence textile collection,
▼ designed by Alfredo Pizzo Greco
   for Mateb, consists of printed silk
   and cotton fabrics and was
   introduced in 1986

■ Patterns in the Armonia collection
   of textiles, introduced by Mario
   Sirtori in 1987, are an homage to
   the artist Paul Klee.

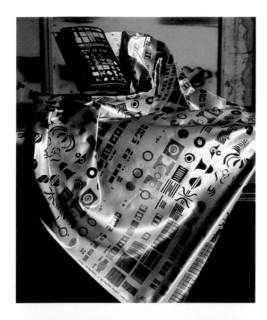

■ Franco Albini's Luisa armchair was designed in 1951 for Poggi. It has a rosewood frame and upholstered seat and back.

■ The Genni lounge chair, designed in 1934 by Gabriele Mucchi, was reintroduced by Zanotta in 1982.

▼ Enzo Mari designed the Tonietta chair, introduced by Zanotta in 1985. The chair has an aluminum alloy frame, with seat and back covered in stiff cowhide.

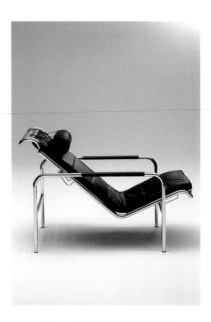

■ Gino Levi Montalcini, embracing the Bauhaus aesthetic, designed the Germana cantilevered chair in 1928. Zanotta reissued it in 1976.

■ Giò Ponti was inspired by the vernacular chair designs of Chiavari in creating the Superleggera 699 side chair, introduced in 1957 by Cassina.

▼ The Follia, a 1934 Giuseppe Terragni chair design, produced since 1972 by Zanotta, has a black wooden seat and back with distinctive chrome-plated steel leaf-spring supports.

■ Nuova X-Line stacking chair, with perforated metal seat and back, was designed in-house by Magis and introduced in 1979.

■ The Fiera di Trieste wooden folding chair was designed in 1966 for Alberto Bazzani by Pierangelo D'Aniello and Aldo Jacober.

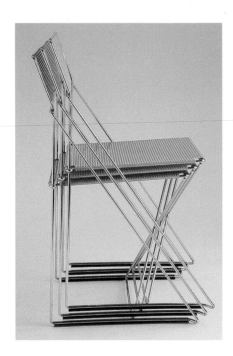

■ The Blitz, a metal and flexible
▼ polyurethane folding chair, was
designed by Motomi Kawakami for
Skipper in 1977.

■ The adjustable Talao high chair
folds for storage and can be used
as a conventional chair. It was
designed by the Zetass Studio in
1978 and is manufactured by
Norda Tubazioni

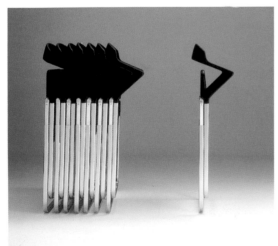

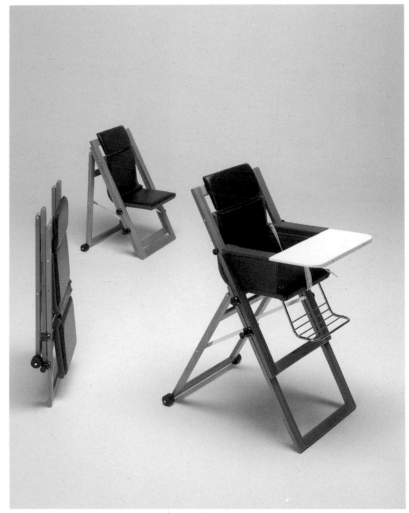

■ Kartell's 4800 stools have a seat made of molded polyurethane with legs and backs in tubular metal. The stools were designed by Anna Castelli Ferrieri in 1979.

▼ The Trio, a table/valet stand in tubular steel and ABS plastic, was designed in 1980 by Roberto Lucci and Paolo Orlandini for Magis.

■ The molded polyurethane seat of the 4800 stool series was designed for simple insertion of metal tube legs and back handle, without the need for complicated connecting bolts or screws.

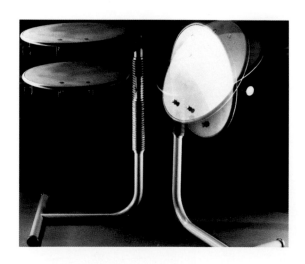

■ The 5340 steel and canvas cot is
▼ part of a line of nursery school furnishings designed by Centrokappa
and manufactured by Kartell since
1978.

■ Achille and Pier Giacomo Castiglioni's 1957 Mezzadro stool incorporates a standard tractor seat on
a cantilevered base of steel and
wood. It has been manufactured
since 1970 by Zanotta.

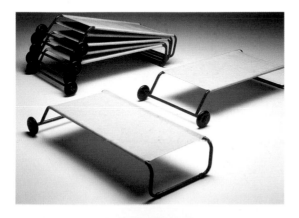

■ The Veranda seating series, designed by Vico Magistretti in 1983, features folding back, arm and footrest elements. It is manufactured by Cassina.

■ Two-seat Veranda models, show-
▼ ing the various positions the chairs can be placed in for individual seating comfort.

■ Michelle De Lucchi's First chair was introduced as part of the Memphis line of 1983. The chair offers the signature avant-garde shapes and colors associated with Memphis, but also addresses the concept of mass production, as it is simply constructed and rather tame in comparison to more outlandish, one-of-a-kind Memphis creations.

■ The Fiocco chair consists of a piece of elastic fabric stretched over a tubular metal frame. It was designed in 1970 by Gianni Pareschi for Busnelli.

▼ Gaetano Pesce's New York Sunset, a humorous soft-sculpture sofa designed in 1980, is manufactured by Cassina.

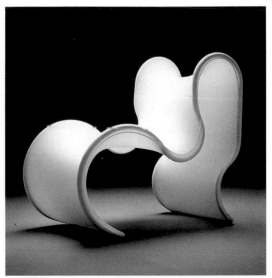

■ Designed in 1968 by Gatti, Paolini, Teodoro, the Sacco chair, often called the ''bean bag,'' is a soft leather ''ball'' filled with polystyrene pellets. Manufacturer: Zanotta.

■ The Vanity Fair armchair has been produced by Poltrona Frau since 1930.

■ The adjustable Itaca lounge chair, designed by Nilo Gioacchini and Luca Pettinari in 1985, includes attached side table and reading light. Manufacturer: Arflex.

■ The Eva, a side chair designed by Paolo Nava for Flexform in 1982, consists of a simple metal structure "clothed" in a fabric "dress."

▼ The Armchair in Three Pieces was designed in 1952 by Franco Albini, Franca Helg and Paolo Piva. Produced by Poggi, the chair has a tubular steel frame.

■ The steel Seconda chair, designed by Mario Botta and produced by Alias in 1981, has a rotating rubber "pillow."

■ Rudi Dordoni designed the Lipsia chairs and tables in 1984. The lacquered metal furniture line is manufactured by Cappellini International.

■ The Delfina stacking chair, combining a tubular steel frame and anodized aluminum seat and backrest, was designed in 1974 by Enzo Mari for Driade.

■ The Teatro chair series was designed by Luca Meda and Aldo Rossi for Molteni in 1981.

▼ Thin strands of PVC make up the "upholstery" of the aptly named Spaghetti chair, designed by Giandomenico Belotti for Alias in 1979.

■ The Tomasa, a folding wood chair designed in the 15th Century by Paolo Uccello, is manufactured by Simon.

■ The Miamina, a portable chair, consists of eight tubes which are fitted into a central joint and covered by a piece of fabric. The entire chair can be taken apart and placed in a carrying bag. The chair "concept" was designed by Alberto Salvati and Ambrogio Tresoldi and is manufactured by Saporiti Italia.

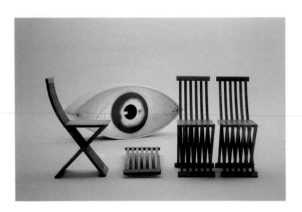

■ Joe, the ultimate "Pop" armchair, is an homage to baseball player Joe DiMaggio and was designed in 1970 by Jonathan De Pas, Donato D'Urbino and Paolo Lomazzi for Poltronova.

■ Sergio Mazza's Toga armchair is formed from a single piece of reinforced plastic resin. It was designed in 1969 and is manufactured by Artemide.

LIGHTING

■ The Saori series of square, rectangular and oval wall lights was designed in 1973 by Kazuhide Takahama for Sirrah. Light is diffused through a washable, heat-resistant fabric shade.

■ Tobia Scarpa's 1973 Quarto sconce is manufactured by Flos.

▼ The Foglio sconce, manufactured by Flos, was designed in 1966 by Tobia Scarpa.

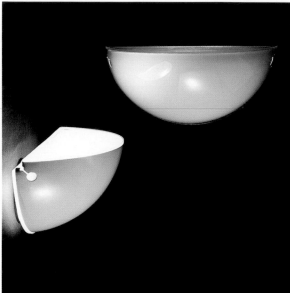

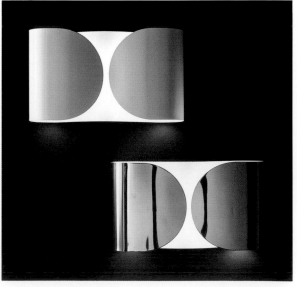

■ The swing-arm 265 wall lamp, designed in 1973 by Paolo Rizzatto, is produced by Arteluce.

■ Designed by Tobia Scarpa in 1973 and introduced by Flos in 1977, the Ariette 3 wall or ceiling fixture has a synthetic fabric diffuser.

■ The Plek ceiling fixture, designed
by Jeannot Cerrutti in 1986, is
manufactured by Veart.

■ The Luceplan Trama suspension
light, designed by Luciano Bales-
trini and Paola Longhi in 1985, can
be raised and lowered by its integrated counterweight system.

■ The Expanded Line Network, an
Arteluce product designed by King
Miranda Associates in 1983, is an
integrated lighting system based
on tubular modules from which a
series of fixtures and accessories
can be hung. Both fluorescent and
incandescent sources can be used
with the system.

■ The Zoom hanging lamp, designed
by Jeannot Cerutti in 1986, is
manufactured by Veart.

■ Jeannot Cerutti designed the Doremi hanging lamp in 1986 for Veart.

▼ The F1 suspension lamp was designed for Luceplan in 1982 by Paolo Rizzatto.

■ Achille Castiglioni and Pio Manzù designed the Parentesi light in 1970 for Flos. A spotlight, attached to a metal tube, can be moved vertically along the weighted steel cable that is hung from the ceiling.

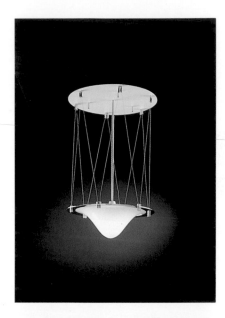

■ Designed by Maurizio Bertoni in 1983, the Lippa, manufactured by Castaldi, is a swing-arm ceiling or wall fixture.

■ Sirrah's Diskos, designed by Giovanni Offredi in 1983, is a pendant lamp constructed of ABS plastic with a translucent Vedril diffuser.

▼ The Euclide was designed in 1986 by Maurizio Ferrari. Manufactured by Luceplan, the hanging lamp has a sandblasted glass diffuser.

■ Crisol, a suspension lamp with colored, etched glass diffuser, was designed in 1981 by Perry King, Santiago Miranda and Gianluigi Arnaldi for Arteluce.

▼ Altalite's Structura system, based on a modular metal space frame to which lighting and other electrical devices can be attached, was introduced by the firm in 1978.

■ King Miranda Associates' Aurora suspension lamp consists of three cone-shaped diffusers placed in a layered crystal disk that glows, as it too diffuses light. The fixture was introduced in 1983 by Arteluce.

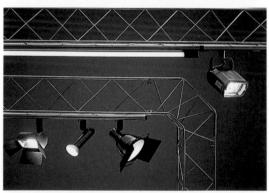

■ Direct and indirect lighting is provided by the Halley suspension lamp, designed in 1980 by Perry King, Santiago Miranda and Gianluigi Arnaldi and manufactured by Arteluce.

■ The classic Frisbi suspension lamp, designed by Achille Castiglioni in 1978 and manufactured by Flos, provides three types of light: direct, diffused and indirect.

▼ The Splügen Braü, a pendant lamp, was designed by the Castiglionis in 1961. It is manufactured by Flos.

■ The Arco, designed in 1962 by Achille and Pier Giacomo Castiglioni for Flos, has a Carrara marble base, stainless-steel arm and polished aluminum reflector.

▼ Gregotti Associates' Segno Uno, designed in 1981 for Fontana Arte, has a base and stem in varnished metal, shade and bowl in blown glass.

■ The Gibigiana floor or table lamp, designed in 1980 by the Castiglionis for Flos, has an adjustable reflector to regulate the amount of light desired.

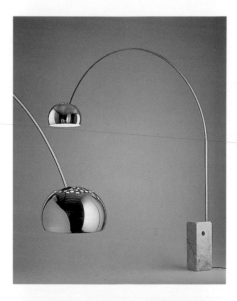

■ The Musa, a torchere designed by
Maurizio Peregalli for Zeus/Noto in
1985, has a painted steel stem and
ceramic head.

■ The Luminator, designed by
Luciano Baldessari in 1929, is
manufactured by Luceplan. The
winding tube around the cylinder is
designed to move, to symbolize
the graceful turning of a ballerina in
motion.

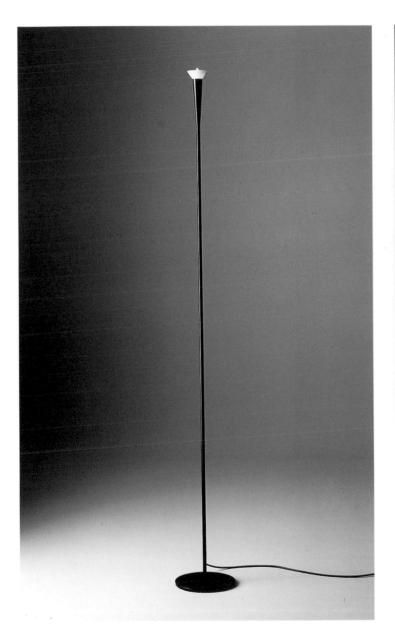

■ The Jill torchere was designed in 1978 by Perry King, Santiago Miranda and Gianluigi Arnaldi. Manufactured by Arteluce, the lamp has an etched glass diffuser and base, offered in various hues.

▼ The Toio floor lamp, designed by the Castiglionis in 1962, is manufactured by Flos.

■ Designed in 1984 by Asahara Sigheaki, the Palomar torchere is manufactured by Stilnovo.

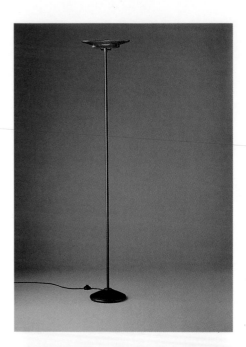

■ Tobia Scarpa's Perpetua lamp has an adjustable diffuser set into a metal track. It was designed in 1982 and is manufactured by Flos.

■ Pietro Chiesa designed the Luminator in 1933. Its classic design has inspired many other designers throughout the latter half of the 20th century. Manufacturer: Fontana Arte.

▼ The Tortuga watertight lamp is designed for use outdoors. Manufactured by Castaldi in 1979, it was designed by Maurizio Bertoni.

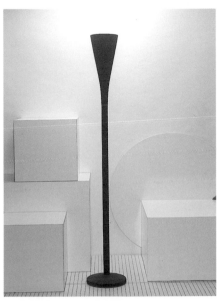

■ The Spider clamp table light,
designed by Joe Colombo in 1966,
is manufactured by Oluce. The first
prototype of the lamp, used in
Colombo's own office, is finished
in chrome, as he wished it to be
produced. For marketing reasons,
today it is produced in nine color
finishes.

■ Paolo Rizzatto's 612/3 adjustable
task lamp was designed in 1975
for Arteluce.

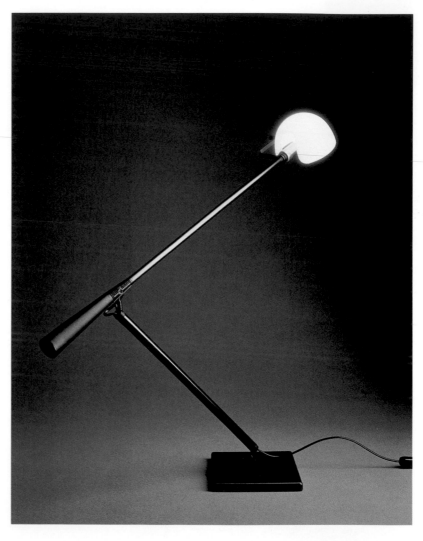

■ The Berenice desk lamp was designed in 1985 by Paolo Rizzatto and Alberto Meda. It is manufactured by Luceplan.

▼ Luceplan's Costanza table lamp is Paolo Rizzatto's updated version of a classic form. It was designed in 1987.

■ The dramatic Taccia table lamp, designed by the Castiglionis in 1962, is manufactured by Flos. Its glass diffuser is reminiscent of ancient Tuscan glassware, while its base form is inspired by the shape of a gas burner.

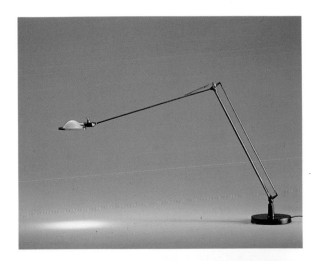

■ The Orsolo, a metal table lamp, was designed by Stefano Panichi in 1986 for Quattrifolio.

■ A "pop" design of 1987, the Graffa
▼ folding desk lamp by Claudio Nordio is an electrified paper clip. Manufacturer: Quattrifolio.

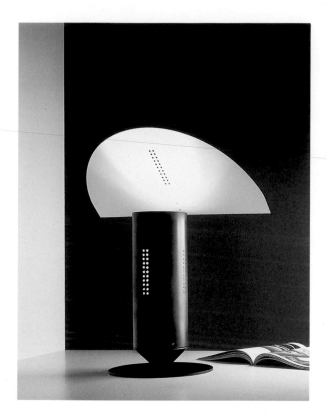

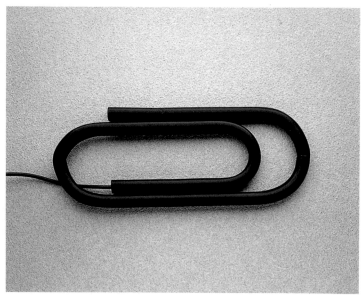

■ An adjustable, multicolored plastic arm distinguishes the Nastro desk lamp, designed in 1983 for Stilnovo by Alberto Fraser. *Nastro* means ''ribbon'' in Italian.

■ Made entirely of glass, the Fatua table lamp was designed for Fontana Arte by Guido Rosati in 1970.

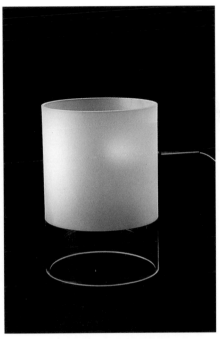

■ The Daphine table lamp has an
exposed transformer as its base. It
was designed for Lumina by
Tommaso Cimini in 1978.

▼ The No. 1 series of lamps was
designed by Giovanni Albera and
Nicolas Monti in 1984. No. 1 can
be used as a table lamp or, with an
extension arm, as a floor lamp.
Manufacturer: S.I.D.I.

■ De Pas, D'Urbino, Lomazzi's
Lucifero table lamp, with adjustable
metal reflector, was designed in
1982 and is manufactured by
Bilumen.

■ The Atollo, a lacquered aluminum table lamp, was designed in 1976 for Oluce by Bruno Gecchelin.

▼ The Alba and Albina table lamp models were designed in 1981 by Giuliana Gramigna for Quattrifolio.

■ Designed in 1973 by De Pas, D'Urbino, Lomazzi, the Maniglia lamp is manufactured by Stilnovo. *Maniglia* means "handle" in Italian.

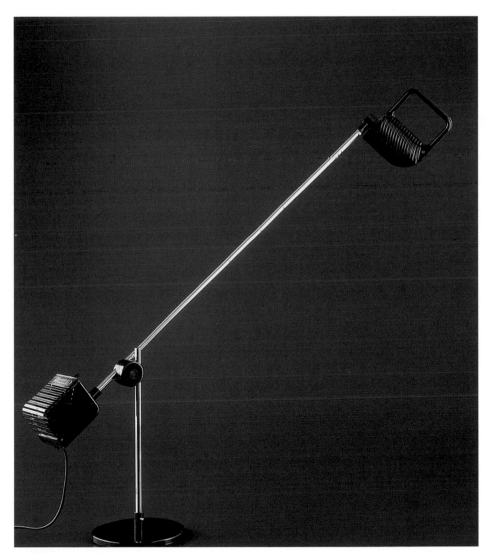

STORAGE

■ The Aforismi line of storage units, with sliding tambour doors, was designed by Antonia Astori in 1983–84 for Driade. The cabinets have a textured metallic paint finish.

■ The Sole Mio shelf, designed by Lodovico Acerbis and Giotto Stoppino in 1982–83, and introduced by Acerbis International, has an attached mirror which can be positioned as desired.

▼ Sergio Mazza's Bacco, an ABS plastic cocktail cabinet on wheels, was designed in 1967–69 for Artemide.

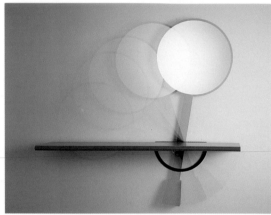

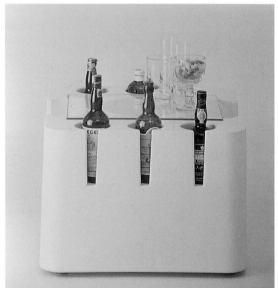

■ The Playbox, a Lodovico Acerbis and Giotto Stoppino design of 1984, consists of two separate cabinets placed side by side. The storage units are manufactured by Acerbis International.

▼ De Pas, D'Urbino, Lomazzi's Sciangai clothes rack, designed in 1973–74 for Zanotta, is made of beechwood and can be folded for storage.

■ The interior configuration of a Playbox, containing a small bar, television and audio equipment.

▼ Enzo Mari's Tricorno hat rack, made of enameled steel poles with brightly colored plastic clothes hooks, was designed in 1980 and is manufactured by Danese.

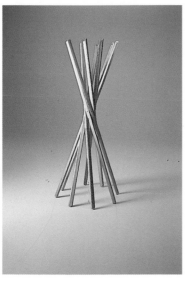

■ The Serranda Odeon storage
component system can be
configured in various ways. The
system was designed in 1986–87
by Carlo Bartoli for Arc Linea.

■ Vico Magistretti's 1977 Nuvola
▼ Rossa shelving system for Cassina
is based on the rather simple
concept of placing "boards" on the
rungs of stylized "ladders." All
elements in the system are made
of beechwood.

Kaos, an Antonia Astori-designed storage system, features vertical panels onto which shelving, overhead storage units, cabinets, table surfaces and other elements can be attached. The flexible system was designed in 1985–86 for Driade.

Andries and Hiroko Van Onck designed the King 2 receptacle in 1985–86. Manufactured by Magis, the ABS plastic tube can be covered with a melamine ashtray element.

■ The Joint shelving system, designed by Luciano Pagani and Angelo Perversi in 1985, consists of a tubular metal frame, onto which rubber-covered, bendable hooks are attached to support glass shelves.

▼ Afra and Tobia Scarpa's Accademia chest of drawers, executed in walnut, was designed in 1975–77 and manufactured by Stildomus.

■ Storage elements from the
▼ Roberto Volonterio and Cesare Benedetti-designed Forum furniture system for Bernini, introduced in 1985–86. The units are made of lacquered wood with doors in contrasting pearwood.

■ Kartell's 4962/4 rectangular stacking unit, designed by Olaf von Bohr in 1974, offers dust-free storage capability. No screws or tools are required to assemble or combine units.

▼ The Dedalo umbrella stand, manufactured by Artemide, is made of molded ABS plastic and was designed in 1966 by Emma Schweinberger.

■ The 4953 series of circular stacking units of ABS plastic, part of Kartell's extensive range of simple, sturdy and modular storage pieces, designed in 1969 by Anna Castelli Ferrieri. The inexpensive storage units are produced in bright hues.

■ The Battista, a folding clothing rack designed in 1980–82 by Giuseppe Raimondi for Skipper, is reminiscent of a photographer's tripod.

■ The Sisamo closet system, designed by Kairos in 1983, is equipped with a patented door hinge that allows the doors to slide between units for full access to interior compartments. Manufacturer: B&B Italia.

▼ Double Face, a pivoting bookcase designed by Cini Boeri in 1980–81, is manufactured by Arflex.

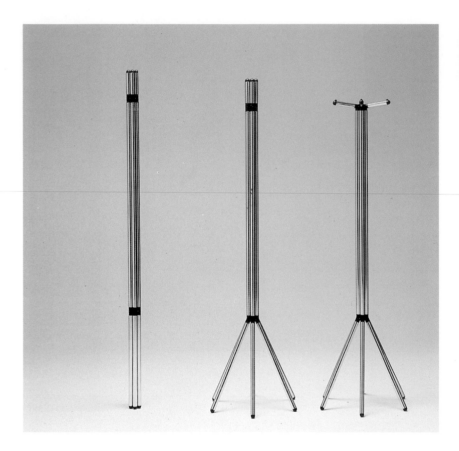

■ The Atlante series of fixed-wall shelving units was designed in 1980 by Giulio Cappellini and Rudi Dordoni for Cappellini.

▼ Franco Raggi's Gelosia sectional bookcase was designed in 1987 for Fontana Arte.

■ Designed in 1986 by Luca Meda for Molteni, the 505 system of storage furniture offers the flexibility of modularity and a look of permanence.

▼ Built like International-style skyscrapers, the Chelidon line of vitrines was designed by the Rimadesio studio in 1986.

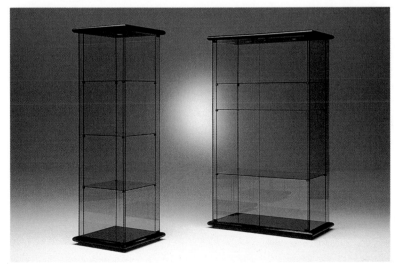

TABLEWARE

■ Lino Sabattini designed the Pale silver serving utensils, produced by the Sabattini factory in 1973.

■ Designed in 1981, Achille Castiglioni's Dry stainless-steel cutlery is produced by Alessi.

▼ The Meridiana series of carving instruments, made of colored methacrylate and stainless steel, was designed by Bruno Gecchelin in 1985 and is produced by Rede Guzzini.

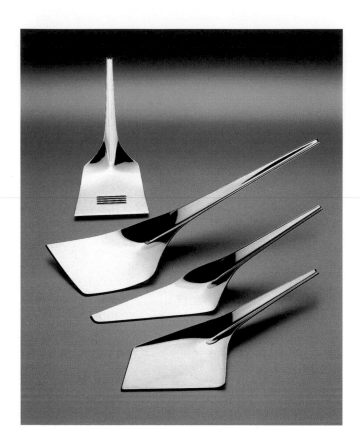

■ Silver carving fork and knife, produced by Cleto Munari, was designed in 1979–80 by Vico Magistretti.

▼ The Instrumenta series of stainless-steel flatware, produced by the Sabattini factory, was designed in 1978 by Lino Sabattini.

■ The Mestoli line of stainless-steel and beechwood kitchen utensils was designed in 1979 by Silvio Coppola for ICM.

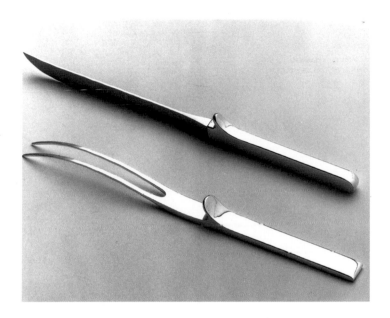

■ Designed from 1985–87, Bruno Gecchelin's bowls, cheese dome, ladles and other utensils, made of layered sheets of colored and transparent methacrylate, are manufactured by Rede Guzzini.

▼ The Rialto collection of Murano glassware, produced by Rede Guzzini, was designed in 1986 by Bruno Gecchelin.

■ The Meridiana carafe and ice
▼ bucket combine crystal with layered sheets of colored and transparent methacrylate. The sleek pieces were designed in 1985–87 by Bruno Gecchelin for Rede Guzzini.

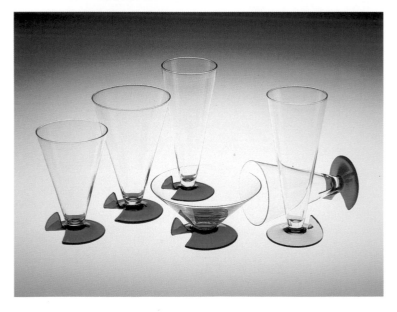

■ Part of the 1982 Memphis collection, the Arturo glass was designed by Marco Zanini.

▼ Ettore Sottsass, Jr. designed the Murmansk silver fruit dish in 1982 for Memphis.

■ Andrea Branzi's 1982 Labrador gravy boat for Memphis, in silver and crystal, reflects the two-sided soul of the designer. A decorative pattern (the "branch") is combined with a classic geometric shape (the "cone").

▼ Paro lead-crystal goblets, designed in 1983 by Achille Castiglioni, are from Danese.

■ Marco Zanini's Vega glass vessel was a 1982 Memphis introduction.

▼ This octagonal flower pot, executed in silver, was designed in 1979 by Carlo Scarpa for Cleto Munari.

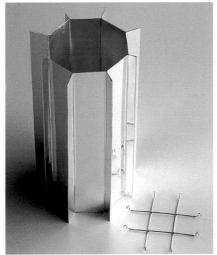

■ The Ice-Stopper drinking glass was designed in 1986 by Angelo Mangiarotti for Colle.

▼ The Olpe crystal cruet set, designed for Collè by Mangiarotti in 1986, has a form that is intended as a reminder of what purpose the objects serve.

■ Mangiarotti's Bibulo series of
▼ decanters and carafes, designed for Colle from 1986–88, are attempts by the designer to relate form to content. The instability of the liquid contained in such objects is reflected in the forms of the objects themselves.

■ The Cartoccio collection of vases, made of Murano glass, was designed in 1984 by Carlo Moretti for his own firm.

■ Carlo Moretti's Rosa Sfumato Verde series of Murano glass drinking glasses and decanters was designed in 1984.

▼ These Murano glass and chrome-plated brass vessels were designed in 1985 by Patrizia Scarzella and Maria Christina Hamel for Carlo Moretti.

■ The Ca'Nova series of pitchers, made of clear acrylic and ABS plastic, was designed in 1985 by Enrico D'Alto for Tre Ti.

■ Richard Sapper's 1982 teapot, designed for Alessi, offers a whimsical three-note whistle operated by the steam pressure created by boiling water.

▼ The La Conica espresso pots, designed by architect Aldo Rossi for Alessi in 1982–84, are reflective of the buildings he has designed. Rossi's intention is to create a "landscape" on the table.

■ The Program for the Majestic Table series, by Materassi and Castaldi for Mas, includes a cruet stand, grated cheese container and salt and pepper shakers held in a metal stand reminiscent of a test-tube holder.

■ The Pasta Set, consisting of a multipurpose boiling pot and steamer in stainless steel, was designed in 1985 by Massimo Morozzi.

▼ Achille Castiglioni's cruet set and salt and pepper shaker was designed in 1980–84 and manufactured by Alessi, a company which has made a point of employing some of the greatest names in design.

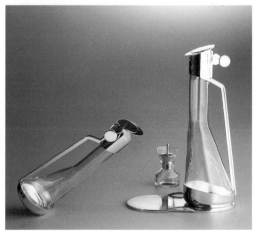

■ Marco Zanuso designed this silver coffee/tea service in 1981 for Cleto Munari.

▼ The Opasis series of electrically welded, mirrored-steel table vessels was designed for Zani in 1986 by Enzo Mari.

■ The 9090 Espresso pot was designed in 1978 by Richard Sapper for Alessi.

▼ The Patrini Due line of drinking glasses, designed by Giovanni Patrini for Cenedese & Albarelli in 1987.

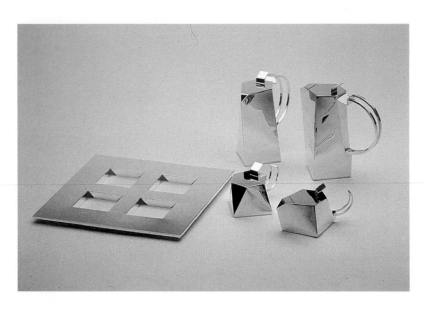

■ A sterling silver teapot with Bakelite handles, designed by Handler Rosenberg, was first produced in 1984 by Pomellato.

▼ Rosenberg's 1982 design for a creamer, sugar bowl and tray.

■ Sterling silver sugar bowl and tea strainer designed by Handler Rosenberg in 1986–87.

▼ Cigarette case and two varieties of cream/sugar sets, designed by Rosenberg in 1982–83.

■ During the 1920s, Paolo Venini founded his glassworks, located on the island of Murano in the Venetian Lagoon. The 1950 Incalmo bottles are classic examples of the innovative output of the Venini factory. They are made by welding two hot-blown glass objects together in order to obtain different color zones in the same object.

■ This Venini-produced series of vessels was designed in 1982 by Laura De Santillana.

▼ The 1948 Alboino vase was first produced by Venini in 1948. It is a Tina Aufiero design.

■ Birgitta and Karllson Öve Thorsen designed the swirled glass Piume vessel for Venini in 1972. *Piume* means "feathers" in Italian.

▼ The Moriandiane series of bottles was first produced by Venini in 1950.

■ The "Paper Bag" vase was designed in 1936 by Pietro Chiesa, Jr. for Fontana Arte.

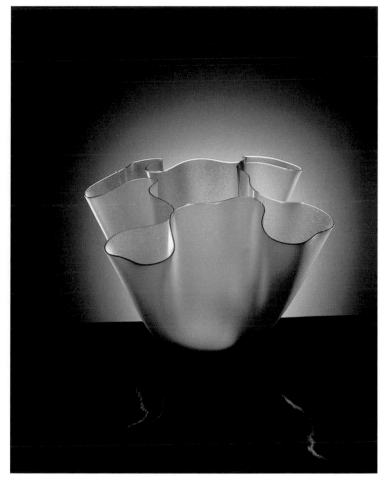

■ Cruet and cheese shaker stand,
part of Materassi and Castaldi's
Majestic program for the Table,
designed in 1984–85 and
manufactured by Mas.

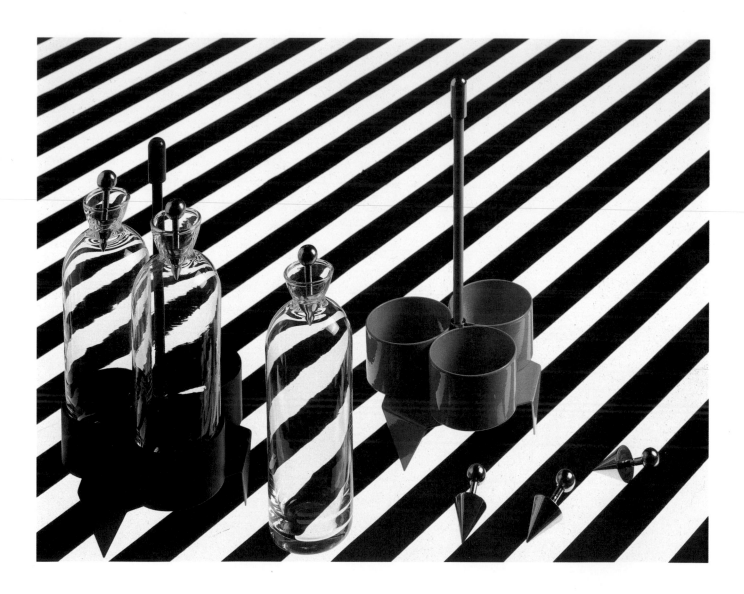

■ The Giotto can-opener was designed in 1986 by Davide Mercatali and Paolo Pedrizzetti for ICOM.

▼ The Center Line series of cookware was designed from 1965 to 1971 by Roberto Sambonet. The stainless-steel pots, pans and serving dishes are manufactured by Sambonet.

■ The Le Pentole set of stackable stainless-steel cooking pans was designed by Niki Sala in 1979 for ICM.

■ Filippo Alison's 1985–86 Filumena 2 Neapolitan coffee pot, produced by Sabattini, has a form reflective of the traditional coffee pot of southern Italy.

■ Lino Sabattini's Estro gravy boat was designed in 1976–77.

▼ The Boule silver teapot was designed in 1950 by Lino Sabattini.

■ The Como tea and coffee service, designed in 1957, is by Lino Sabattini.

■ The Concerto, a three-part silver vase, was designed in 1960 by Lino Sabattini.

▼ A 1979 Lino Sabattini design, the Centro fruit bowl is silver, with tubular metal handle.

APPLIANCES

■ Ariston's I-FEVE 9FB electric oven,
▼ designed by Makio Hasuike in
1986, features a pull-out door
handle to retain flat surface when
not in use.

■ The Margherita washing machine,
a 1983 Makio Hasuike design, is
manufactured by Ariston.

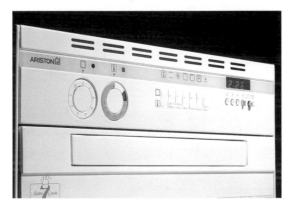

■ Sleek built-in oven chamber is part
of The Wizard's Collection
designed in 1988 by Roberto
Pezzetta for Zanussi.

■ The Wizard's Collection cooktop,
by Roberto Pezzetta, is a flat
vitreous china surface under which
electric and halogen heating
elements are hidden.

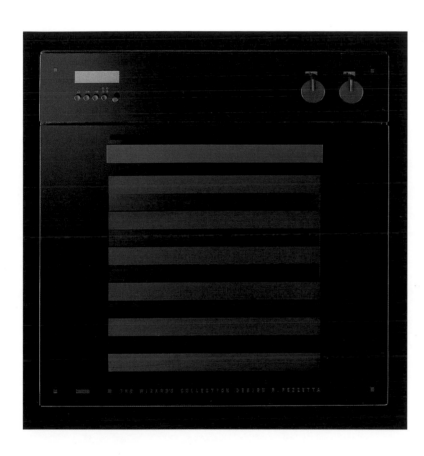

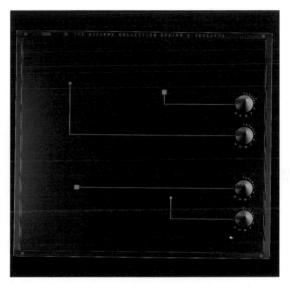

■ The Press-O-Matic is an electronic ironing board that folds flat for carrying. Design Group Italia created the product for Vigorelli in 1980.

■ When ready for use, the carrying handle of the Press-O-Matic ironing board serves as part of its stand.

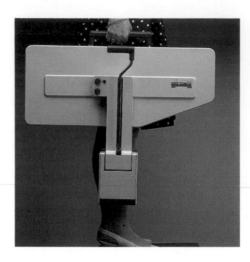

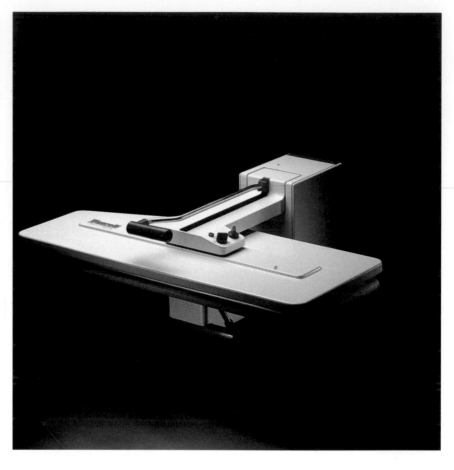

■ The Alfatec 20L vacuum cleaner, designed by Francesco Trabucco and Marcello Vecchi in 1974, incorporates industrially-tested components.

▼ Compact vacuum cleaner is a 1981–82 design by Franceso Trabucco and Marcello Vecchi for Alfatec.

■ Giorgio Giugiaro's Logica electronic sewing machine was designed in 1982. Manufactured by Necchi, the product offers a programmable memory and can produce 100 basic stitches.

▼ The Mirella, a 1957 design by Marcello Nizzoli for Necchi, is a portable sewing machine with built-in extension surface.

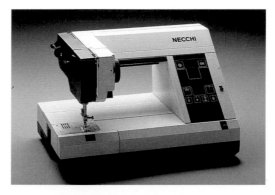

■ The Caldodo Rapid fan/heater, manufactured by Vortice, was designed in 1981 by Francesco Trabucco, Marcello Vecchi and Jesse Marsh.

■ Girmi's Caffe Concerto, designed by Luca Meda in 1983, is a home or office coffeemaker which can also heat water for tea or milk for cappuccino.

■ The Silver A6 coffee grinder, designed by Giuseppe Roccio for Faema in 1986, is equipped with an automatic stop device which prevents over-filling the ground coffee container.

■ The Scaldina fan/heater was designed in 1981 by Gianni Arduini, Lorenzo Bonfanti and Gianfranco Salvemini for BCS Progetti.

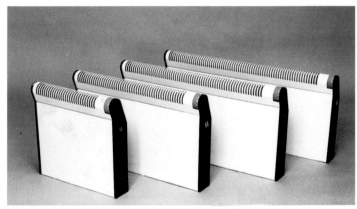

KITCHEN/BATH PRODUCTS

■ Gliding vertical storage unit is part of the Pragma kitchen.

■ The Pragma, designed in 1986–87 by Giovanni Offredi for Mobiam, is a modular kitchen with units offered with wood, laminate, stainless-steel and granite finishes.

■ Antonio Citterio designed Boffi's
▼ Gourmet kitchen, incorporating
elements from professional
kitchens. The 1985 series
combines high-tech stainless steel
with natural beechwood.

■ Snaidero's modular Tempo kitchen,
designed by Michele Sbrogio in
1985, features units covered in
wood veneer and plastic laminate.

■ Designed for the professional kitchen by Luciano Valboni, the H900 cooking unit, in stainless steel, was introduced by Zanussi in 1984.

■ The Panorama 5, a rotisserie unit, manufactured by Zanussi, was designed in 1987 by Luciano Valboni.

▼ The heavy-duty LS/860 dishwasher, designed by Luciano Valboni in 1985, is manufactured by Zanussi.

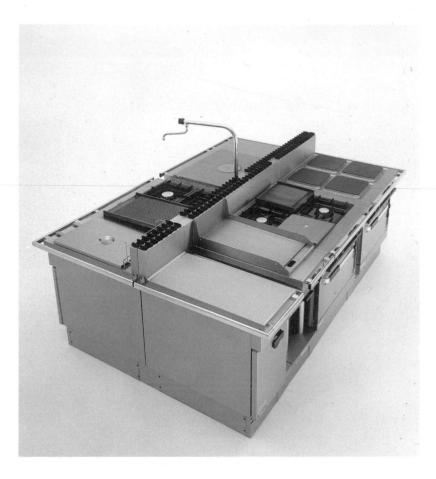

■ The Nuvola kitchen, designed and manufactured by Dada, is a modular series of wooden components covered in laminate, with countertops offered in laminate, marble or granite. The kitchen series was designed in 1981.

▼ Cupboard units of the Nuvola kitchen can be stacked vertically.

■ Snaidero's Idea modular kitchen, designed in 1984 by Michele Sbrogio, can be configured to suit any shape of room. Built-in and freestanding elements are made of chipboard which can be covered in a variety of materials, including lacquered wood and plastic laminate.

■ The FC-10G convection oven, manufactured by Mareno, was designed in 1983 by Bruno Gastaldo. Interior and exterior portions of the unit are covered in stainless steel.

■ The Krios, a modular kitchen, was designed by Giovanni Offredi in 1983–84 and manufactured by Abaco.

▼ The Series 900 stainless-steel cooking center was designed in 1983–84 for Mareno by Bruno Gastaldo.

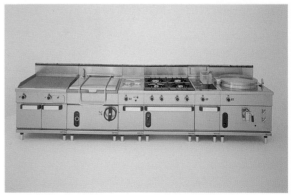

■ The Quinta, a 1985 kitchen design
by Paolo Piva, has a decidedly
postmodern appearance, a
departure from the modernist
vocabulary of similarly constructed
modular kitchen products.
Manufacturer: Dada

■ The Alpes Inox sink, with built-in colander, cutting board and drain board, was designed in 1987 by Domenico Moretto.

▼ Domenico Moretto's 1985 corner stove for Alpes Inox includes conventional burners and gas barbecue.

■ The Kalya kitchen was designed in 1985 by Giovanni Offredi for Abaco.

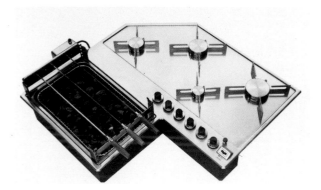

■ All appliance units of the Kalya
kitchen are built-in. The countertop
and backsplash are combined into
a single module.

■ The Weekend, a freestanding
kitchen unit, was designed by
Giulio Manzoni and Flora Crippa
for MG Due in 1983.

■ The Ala Sospesa toilet and bidet, designed by Ideal Standard in 1986, attach to the wall of the bathroom, keeping floor areas open to ease maintenance.

▼ Sink, toilet and bidet are part of the Linda series, designed for Ideal Standard in 1978 by Achille Castiglioni.

■ The Zagara series of sanitary fixtures offer a new shape. The sink, toilet and bidet were designed in 1986 by Marco Zanuso for Ceramica Dolomite.

■ Designed to fit into the space occupied by a standard bathtub, Fred Drugman, Margherita De Carli and Fulvia Premoli's Soluzione hydromassage tub of metacrylate was introduced in 1984 by Jacuzzi Italy.

■ The Drugman/De Carli/Premoli team also designed the Simbolo tub for Jacuzzi in 1984. It is a corner model.

▼ The oversized Diva tub was designed in 1984 by Drugman/De Carli/Premoli for Jacuzzi.

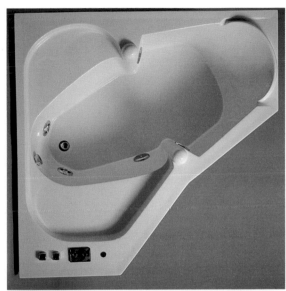

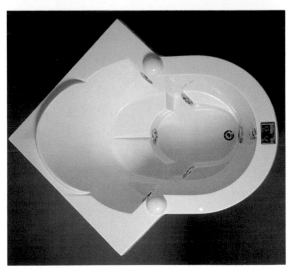

- The Calibro bathtub fixtures, produced by Fantini, were designed in 1982 by Davide Mercatali and Paolo Pedrizzeti.

▼ The single-lever basin faucet, offered in a range of colors, was designed in 1976 by Carlo Santi for Stella.

- Brightly colored tap fixture is part of the I Balocchi line designed in 1979 by Davide Mercatali and Paolo Pedrizzetti for Fantini.

▼ The Genius single-lever tap, designed by Franco Mirenzi in 1985, is manufactured by Sottini.

- Walter Fabian designed the Dualux, a tap fixture with built-in leak control mechanism. It was first manufactured by Ideal Standard in 1979.

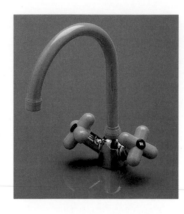

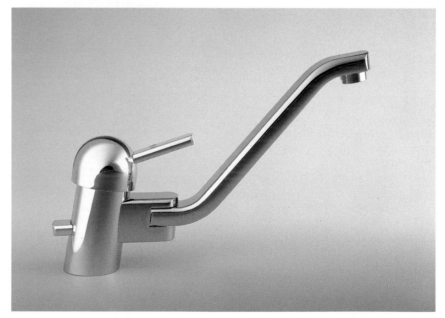

■ Ideal Standard's Class series of faucets was designed in 1987 by Mario Bellini.

▼ Coriandoli bath/shower control, manufactured by Zucchetti, was designed in 1984 by Raul Barbieri and Giorgio Marianelli.

■ The wall-mounted Genius single-lever tap.

▼ The Stella Company's Roma bath/shower fixture was introduced in 1926. Most fixtures from the 1970s and 1980s are merely cosmetic reinterpretations of this functional design.

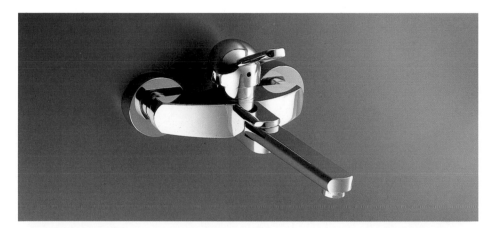

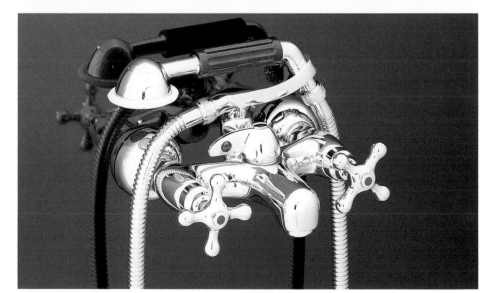

BUILDING ELEMENTS

■ Abet Laminati's Diafos line of plastic laminates takes patterned laminate technology a step further. Designed in 1987, the surfaces are translucent, allowing light to pass through for the creation of new interior effects.

■ Additional patterns in Abet Laminati's Diafos line.

■ Abet's Venice laminates offer surfaces with a velvet or embossed textured finish.

■ Additional patterns from the Diafos translucent laminate line.

▼ Diafos laminate patterns are adapted from standard patterns in the Abet line, including some designed by Ettore Sottsass, Jr.

■ Marble tile pattern, designed by
Luca Scacchetti in 1986, is
composed of yellow and red
Bimarmi marbles. Tiles are
individually bonded.

■ Luca Scacchetti's 1986 marble tile
pattern made up of yellow and red
Bimarmi tiles.

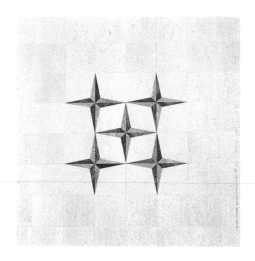

■ Tile pattern by Eugenio Manzoni
made up of Black Marquinia and
red marbles, was first produced by
Bimarmi in 1986.

■ Eugenio Manzoni's patterned tile
design employing white Thassos,
Black Marquinia and green Giulia
marbles.

■ Colorful ceramic tiles, manufactured by Cottoveneto, are offered
in a wide range of shapes and
sizes. Shown are offerings
designed in the 1980s.

■ The Bisanzio collection of ceramic
tiles was designed by Giovanni
Massari and Renato Toso in 1983.
Produced by the Gabbianelli
factory, the tiles are decorated
with a pattern offered in a range of
scales.

▼ A tile from the Bisanzio collection.

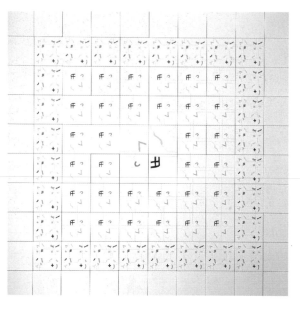

■ Designed in 1985 by Mario Sutor,
the 5 x 5 series consists of
handpainted ceramic tiles.
Manufacturer: Cottoveneto.

■ Harem ceramic tiles, designed by
Anna Maglienti for Gabbianelli in
1982, exhibit the precise color
capability of the Italian ceramic tile
industry.

■ Verbano window handle is part of a series designed by Fabrizio Bianchetti for Olivari in 1983.

■ Marco Zanuso's Series 2Z door hardware collection, designed in 1983, is manufactured by Fusital.

▼ Door handle, designed by Fabrizio Bianchetti is from the 1983 Verbano series produced by Olivari.

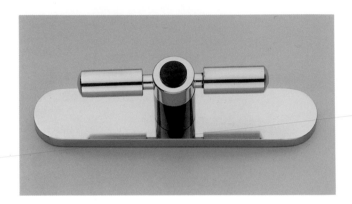

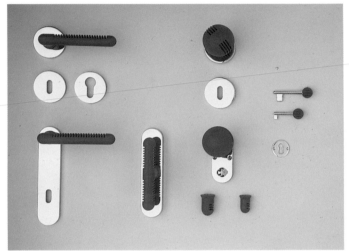

■ The Desipro series of hardware
▼ was designed for use by the
handicapped. Introduced in 1988,
the series was designed for Valli &
Colombo by Attilio Marcolli.

■ The Series 2G, designed by
Gregotti Associates in 1983, is a
coordinated line of door hardware.
Manufacturer: Fusital.

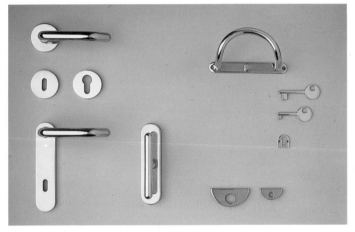

■ Designed by Meroni in 1973, the Premiapri Nova lock for doors offers push-button operation.

■ Tris burled wood door with rounded edges was designed in 1980 by Luigi Caccia Dominioni and is manufactured by Lualdi.

■ Laminate version of the Tris door.

■ The rounded edges of the Tris door
are made of lacquered polyester.

■ The Macco door handle was
designed in 1966 by Sergio Mazza.
Manufacturer: Artemide.

■ Door keys, from the Desipro pro-
▼ gram of hardware for the handicapped, were designed by Attilio
Marcolli for Valli & Colombo.

■ Designed in 1979 by Luigi Caccia
Dominioni, the Monte Carlo door
handle is manufactured by Olivari.

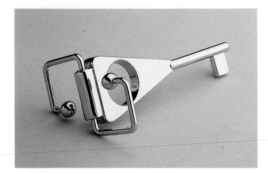

■ The Boma, a door or window handle, was designed in 1972 for Olivari by Gianemilio, Pietro and Anna Monti.

▼ Giò Ponti's Lama door handle of 1956 is manufactured by Olivari.

■ Ambra door handle was designed in 1970 by Franco Albini and Franca Helg for Olivari.

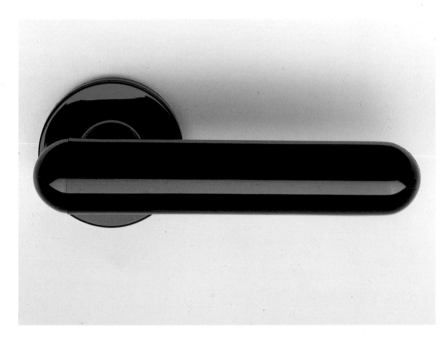

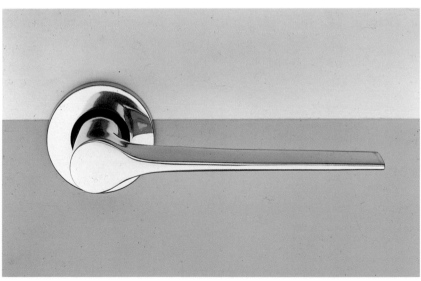

ACCESSORIES

■ Made of melamine plastic, the Spyros ashtray was designed in 1967 by Eleonora Pedruzzi Riva for Artemide.

■ Design Group Italia's 1979 Tratto Clip pen has a synthetic tip.

▼ The Spako string cutter, a product from Design Group Italia, was introduced in 1979. Manufacturer: Domopak.

▼ The Delsopad, a portable clipboard and note pad made of polystyrene and ABS plastic, was designed in 1983 by Arduini Dottori for Delso.

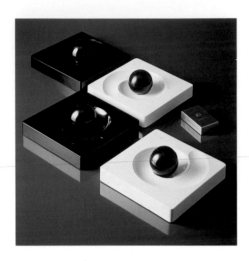

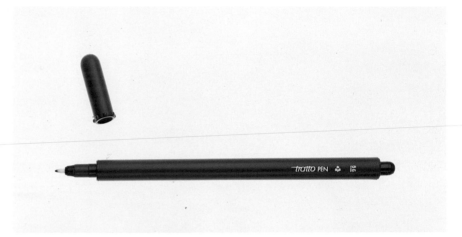

■ The Columbia, designed for Nava by Sottsass Associates in 1980, is a desk diary and supply set.

▼ The Sikuro all-purpose storage element was designed in 1986 by Luigi Massoni and Dino Palizza for Acea. Items are hung from the small rubber pieces that attach to the wall-mounted track.

■ The Aurora Thesi ball-point pen was designed in 1973 by Marco Zanuso

▼ Zanuso's Hastil fountain pen was introduced in 1972 by Aurora.

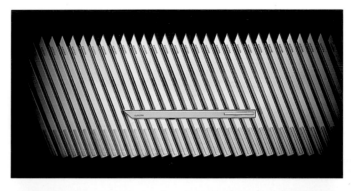

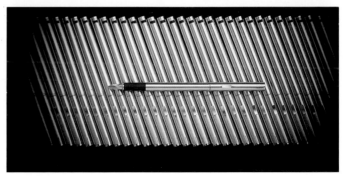

■ The Impronta Z700, designed in 1985 by Makio Hasuike for M.H. Way, is a rucksack made of two semi-rigid plastic fabric shells.

■ Introduced in 1983, the Piuma series of briefcases, drawing cases, notebooks and other types of containers, made of transparent extruded polypropylene, was designed by Makio Hasuike. Manufacturer: M.H. Way.

▼ Zoom, a plastic tube for the transport and storage of drawings, was designed in 1966 by Makio Hasuike for M.H. Way.

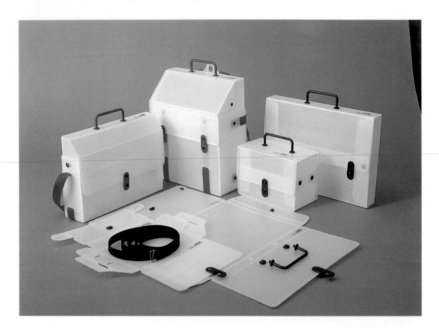

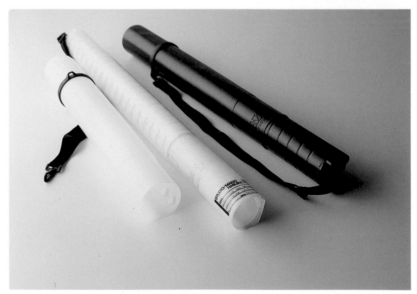

■ The Kartell KS 1068 dust pan, in shock-proof polypropylene, was designed in 1958 by Gino Colombini.

▼ Design Group Italia's Snips scissors, introduced in 1977, are manufactured by Tullen.

■ The Arco, a picture frame, was designed by Giovanni Albera and Marina Clerici in 1985. Manufacturer: Nella Longari.

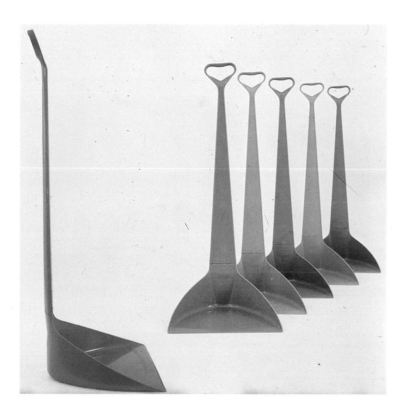

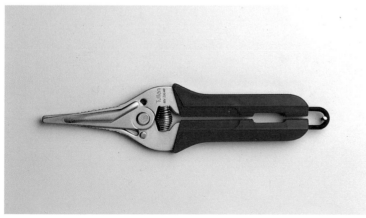

■ The Pivot Plus shaving razor, designed for Schick by Rodolfo Bonetto, was first introduced in 1986.

■ Giovanni Albera and Nicolas Monti designed the Zero ball-point pen in 1985 for S.I.D.I.

▼ The Giglio, an elegantly shaped letter opener produced by Danese, was designed in 1985 by Enzo Mari.

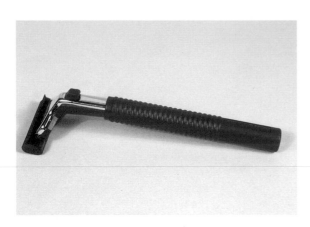

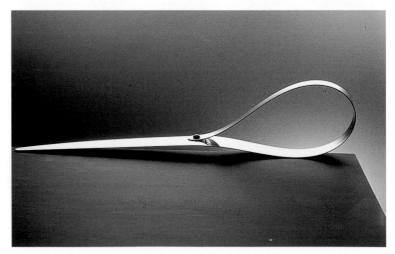

■ Franco Raggi's folding desk clock for Lorenz was designed in 1985.

■ The Danese perpetual calendar, designed in 1967 by Enzo Mari, is made of ABS plastic and PVC.

▼ The Cifra 3 desk clock, with split-flap face, was designed by Gino Valle for Solari Udine in 1965.

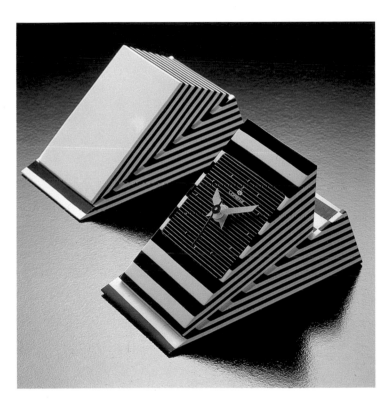

■ The Seiko sports watch collection was introduced in 1982. Giorgio Giugiaro designed the line.

■ The 1985 Lorenz wristwatch line included these models designed by Franco Raggi.

▼ Ettore Sottsass, Jr. designed this gold watch for Cleto Munari in 1986.

■ Franco Raggi's 1985 rhodoid clock was designed for Lorenz.

▼ The Meridiana, a perpetual wall calendar manufactured by Nava, was designed in 1985 by Giulio Confalonieri.

■ Produced by Stilnovo, the 66907 wall clock was designed in 1982 by Asahara Sigheaki.

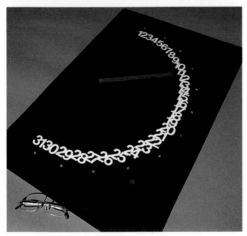

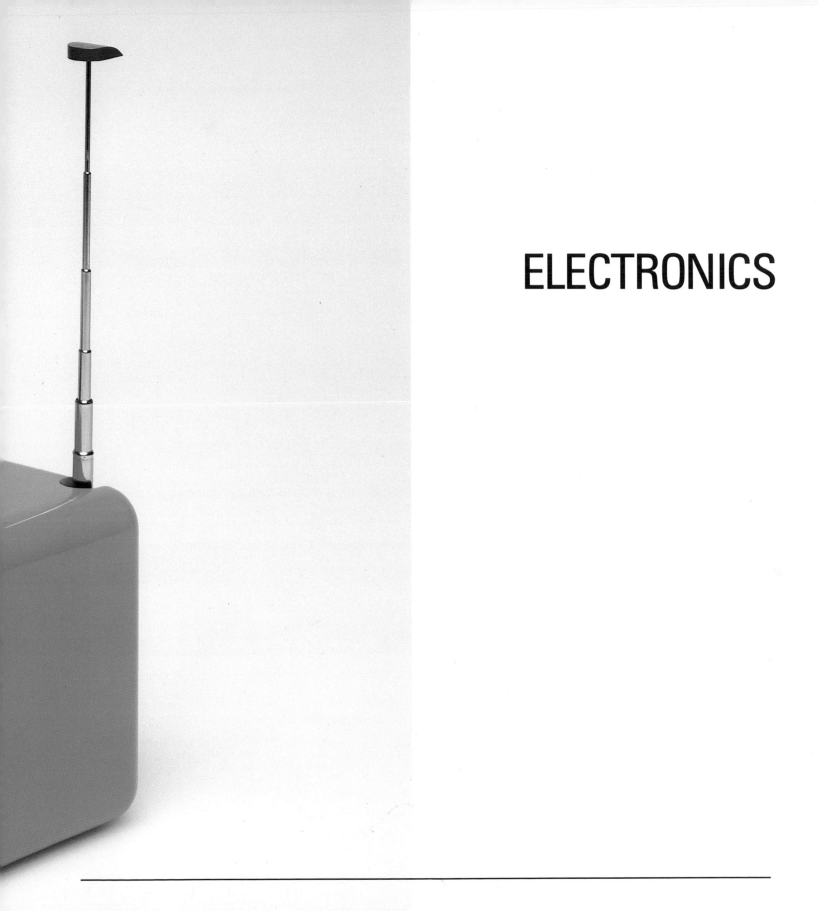

ELECTRONICS

■ Designed by Gianni Pasini and Sandro Pasqui in 1982, the Thema 102 portable computer, with liquid-crystal display panel, flat keyboard, built-in microplotter and mini-printer, is packaged in shock-proof ABS plastic. The state-of-the-art product is produced by IDEA.

■ The E280N, designed by Beppe
▼ Benenti in 1980–81, is an alphanumeric printer for the codification of self-adhesive labels produced by Etipack.

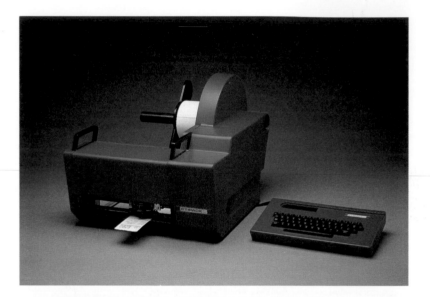

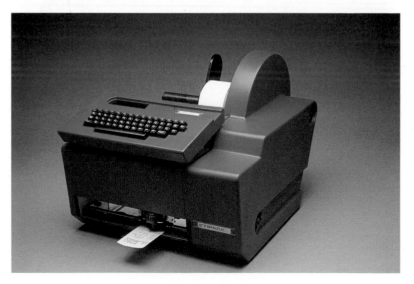

■ Shown installed at the TWA
terminal at Kennedy Airport in New
York City, the flap-unit display
board system was designed in
1961–62 by Gino Valle and is
manufactured by Solari Udine.

■ Gianni Pasini and Sandro Pasqui's one-piece Cobra telephone is crafted of shock-proof ABS plastic and is manufactured by Italtel Telematica.

■ The Rotor public telephone, operated by coin or credit card, was designed by Rodolfo Bonetto in 1986. Manufactured by IPM Napoli, the phone is made of fire-proof plastic and has an armored plexiglass display and a receiver designed to fit into the body of the phone in order to prevent vandalism.

■ Designed by Gianni Pasini and Sandro Pasqui in 1984 for Italtel, the Omega 1000 video display terminal incorporates the Cobra telephone set.

▼ Eumig's Dia Sound System, encased in ABS plastic, is a slide projector with audio capability. The product was designed in 1984 by Nuccio Bertone.

■ The M10/PL10/MC10 portable computer, microplotter and acoustic coupler, from Olivetti, is a compact information system designed by King Miranda in 1983.

■ The Prisma radio-controlled flash-
light, in a brightly colored ABS-plas-
tic shell, manufactured by Reer, is
a 1984 design by Beppe Benenti.

■ Fausta Cavazza's 1985 Parola tele-
▼ phone is made of shock- and
water-resistant Santoprene rubber.
Manufactured by Cavazza Design,
the handset has a built-in shoulder
rest containing a small pencil.

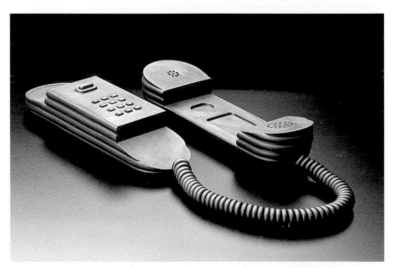

The Algol II portable television set, designed by Marco Zanuso and Richard Sapper, was first introduced in 1962 but is periodically updated to meet the changes needed in form and function. Brionvega, the manufacturer, is currently producing the third generation of this design.

Richard Sapper and Marco Zanuso collaborated on the design of Brionvega's TS 502 portable radio, introduced in 1964. The two-part body is crafted of colorful ABS plastic.

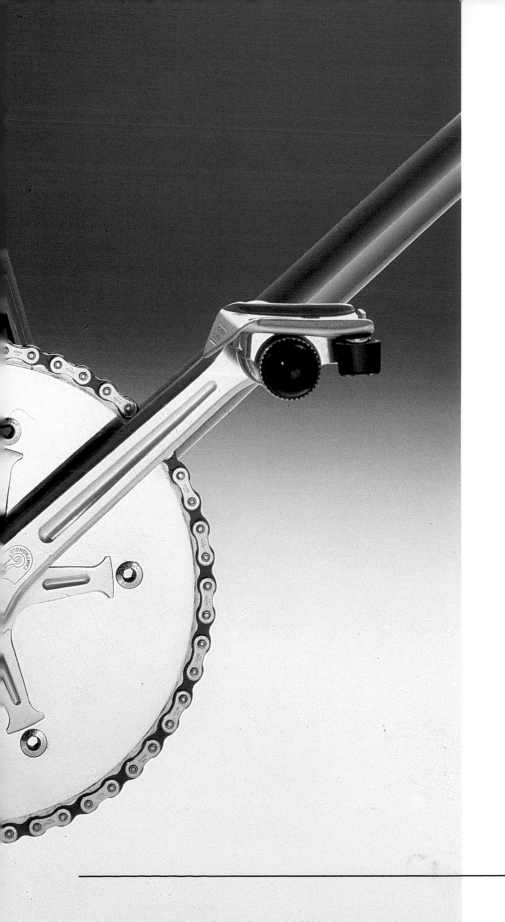

SPORTING EQUIPMENT

■ The Cinelli Laser Pista racing bicycle, designed in 1983, has an aerodynamic form and pared-down appearance. Its frame is made from lightweight steel and its carbon fiber wheels offer less wind resistance.

■ Detail of the streamlined handlebar design of the Laser Pista bicycle.

▼ This Laser Pista model is designed for long-distance races, incorporating derailleur and brakes, yet offering the same lean form.

▼ Detail of the front sprocket of the Laser Pista.

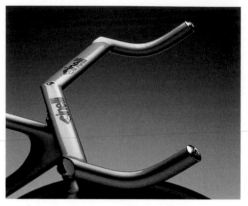

■ The Mattia Esse racing catamaran, with fiberglass-reinforced plastic hull, was designed in 1979 by Enrico Contreas.

▼ Designed for pleasure boating, the Mattia 7.5 catamaran model, first produced in 1985, is an Enrico Contreas design.

▼ Rear view of the Mattia 7.5 catamaran.

■ Nemo marine blocks, designed in 1975 by DA Studio, are updated versions of a usually generic product.

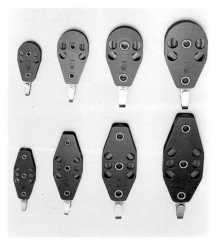

■ Made of polyurethane, the Dolomite ski boot was designed in 1977–78 by Bruno Giardino

■ The Flash rollerskate, designed and produced by F.A.S. in 1985–86, has a transparent zytel sole and lightweight plastic cross straps and wheels.

■ Designed in 1986–87 by F.A.S., the
Leopard rollerskate is made of
black zytel.

■ The Pro XL two-stage diving regulator, designed and manufactured
by Technisub in 1981, is lightweight, with all metal surfaces
shock and corrosion resistant.

■ The Unica fitness machine, incorporating several exercise mechanisms, was designed and manufactured by Technogym in 1987.

■ The seat of the Unica fitness machine adjusts for use by people of differing heights.

▼ The extremely portable and compact 801 mini-sauna, designed in 1986 by Carlo Urbinati for Tecno Guzzini, has an adjustable internal seat, footrest and floor of molded metacrylate and a rubberized canvas enclosure.

■ The Synx 508, designed in 1983 by
▼ Beppe Benenti for Jem, is a
synthesizer. Its electronic
mechanisms are housed in a case
made of sheet steel and
polyurethane.

■ Designed in 1978–79 by Roberto
Lucci and Paolo Orlandini for
Antonelli, the Solista II Concerto
electronic organ can produce the
sound of a variety of musical
instruments. Its simple design
includes color-keyed buttons.

■ The model 804 mountain-climbing pulley with handle, designed by Marco Bonaiti for Kong in 1977–78, is made of stainless steel.

■ The colorful array of yachting, climbing and spelunking snap-links and pulleys were designed from 1945–88 by Marco Bonaiti for Kong.

■ The Maxima Logic tennis racket, designed by Giorgio Giugiaro in 1985–86, is constructed using crisscrossed graphite, ceramic and glass fibers.

■ The Class tennis racket from Maxima features the same composite construction of graphite, ceramic and glass fibers as the Logic model and is also a Giugiaro design.

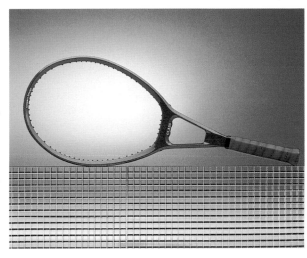

■ The Galaxi F2 diving regulator, manufactured by Cressi-Sub, was designed by the firm in 1978–79.

■ Technisub's Luna Ottica diving mask, designed by the manufacturer in 1986–87, features removable lenses to maintain a clear view underwater.

▼ The NASA swim fin, made of light thermoplastic, is fully flexible. The product was developed in-house at the Technisub design department in 1984–85.

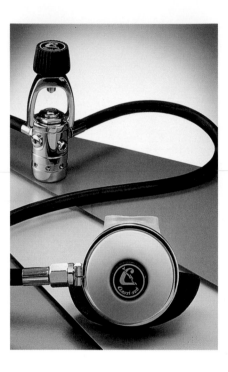

■ Cressi-Sub's 1978–79 Occhio black silicone diving mask is designed for professional use.

▼ The Pinocchio diving mask, from Cressi-Sub, was designed by the company in 1959.

▼ This full-face diving mask, by Cressi-Sub, was introduced in 1960.

■ Designed in 1977, the Piuma 2 diving mask and snorkel, made of rubber, is manufactured by Cressi-Sub.

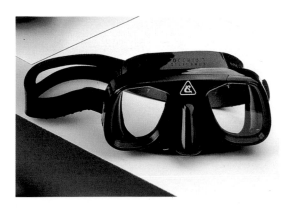

OFFICE FURNITURE

■ The Mixer conference table was
designed by Roberto Pamio for
Arflex in 1984.

■ Solone executive desk and confer-
▼ ence table, designed in 1982 by
Achille Castiglioni for Marcatré,
feature walnut veneer tops and
extruded, aluminum legs with cast-
iron bases.

■ Tecno's Centro Progetti designed the Riunioni T210 conference table in 1981. Top is made of lacquered wood with granite inlay. Legs are made of burnished steel.

■ The Air Mail office chairs, with unusual arm structures, were designed by Perry King and Santiago Miranda for Marcatré in 1985.

■ The Imbottiti 2 WS public seating system from Tecno, introduced in 1981, is a flexible, modular system offered in various configurations. Seats are made of steel wire and are attached to an anchor block of granite.

■ Bench version of the Tecno Imbottiti WS system.

▼ Designed for urban indoor and outdoor settings, the Polis system of steel seating was created by Pier Luigi Molinari for Ambiente International in 1983.

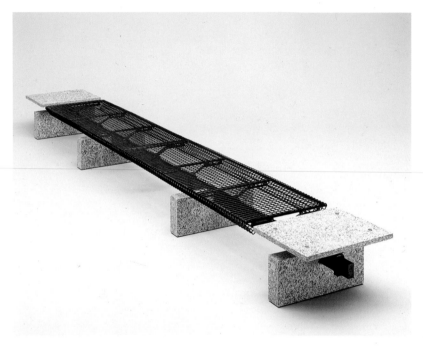

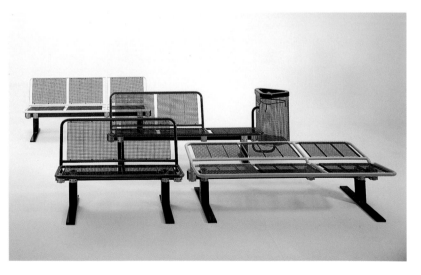

■ Paolo Parigi's Flap folding chair of
▼ 1985–86 has a steel frame with
seat and back made of black
polyurethane foam. Manufacturer:
Parigi Design.

■ These Air Mail chair models, by
King Miranda Associates, were
designed in 1984.

■ The Arcada office furniture system by Paolo Piva, designed in 1985 for B&B Italia, incorporates such precious materials as briarwood and leather into a sleek steel and glass structure.

■ The Arcada office furniture system, shown in an L-shaped configuration.

▼ Olivetti's Spazio office furniture series, designed by the team of Belgiojoso/Peressuti/Rogers in 1961, is a modular system allowing for the creation of desks, shelves and other pieces of furniture.

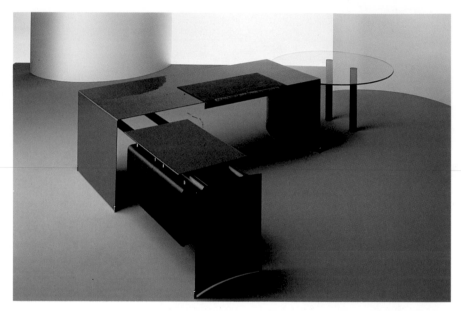

serie SPAZIO   SCRIVANIA S 1613

■ Fantoni D/S furniture, designed by Broggi & Buckhardt Architects, was introduced in 1983. Rich materials such as leather, burled wood and walnut are applied to a modular, electronically adaptable desk system.

■ The Modus 5 System of swivel office chairs, designed and introduced by Tecno in 1971–72, feature pedestal bases of brushed aluminum and seating shells constructed of molded nylon.

■ The Graphis System of desks, conference tables, storage and filing cabinets and partitions, designed for Tecno by Osvaldo Borsani and Eugenio Gerli in 1968.

■ The Satelliti family of supporting
▼ structures for computers, designed
in 1987 by F&L Design for Unifor,
addresses the various needs of the
electronic office, from stands for
personal computers and printers to
the curved workstation designed
specifically for computer graphics
machinery.

■ The Forum Office, designed in
1986 by Roberto Volonterio and
Cesare Benedetti and manufactured by G.B. Bernini, is a series
of writing desks and cabinets
executed in fine lacquered woods.

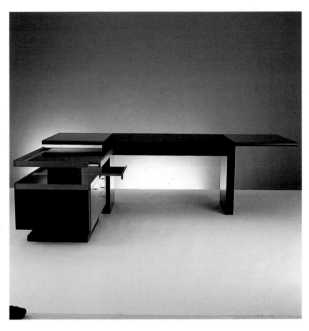

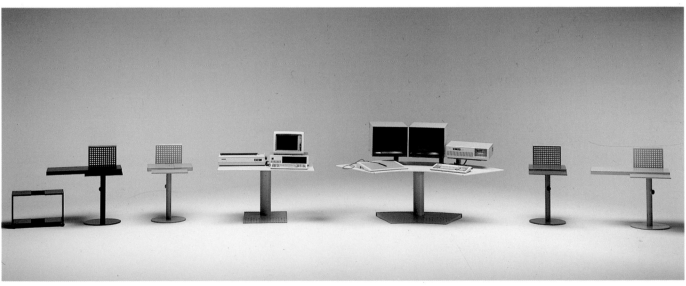

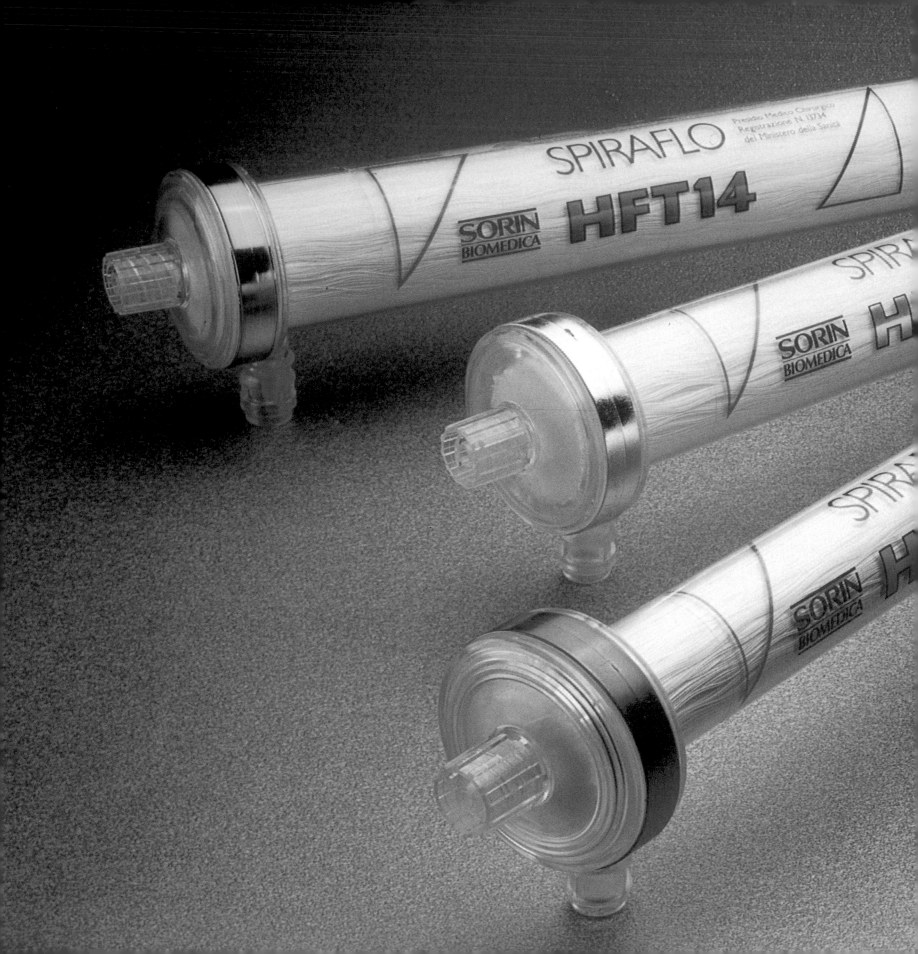

PROFESSIONAL
EQUIPMENT

■ The A90 drawing table, manufactured by Heron Parigi, is a 1975 Paolo Parigi design. Its surface may be raised, tilted or blocked by means of a single pedal.

■ Paolo Parigi's TK/100, designed in 1980, is a precision track-type drawing table manufactured by Heron Parigi.

▼ Giorgio Giugiaro concentrated on the ergonomic aspects of the camera when he designed the Nikon F3, EM and AF camera bodies for Nikon in 1980.

The 988, a variable-speed fan for use in photographic studios, was designed in 1978 for Fatif by Quintino Pina.

Fatif manufactured the DS2 and DS professional cameras in 1970. They were designed by Joe Colombo and Quintino Pina.

■ The 1984 Olivetti personal computers (M10, M20, M21 and M24 models) were designed by Perry King, Antonio Macchi Cassia, Ettore Sottsass, Jr. and George Sowden.

▼ The Programma 101, the first electronic desktop calculator, was designed in 1965 by Mario Bellini for Olivetti.

■ The portable Valentina typewriter, designed by Ettore Sottsass, Jr. in 1965 for Olivetti, had a new, dashing and unconventional air when it was introduced.

▼ Mario Bellini's 1973 Divisumma 18 portable electronic printing calculator, produced by Olivetti, has a keyboard protected by a rubber skin.

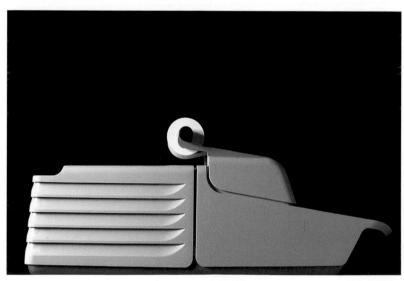

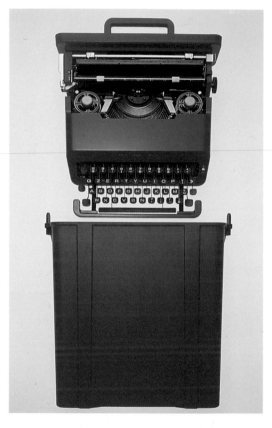

■ The Divisumma 26, designed by Mario Bellini in 1973, is a desktop calculator manufactured by Olivetti.

▼ The Logos 7, a 1978 Mario Bellini design for Olivetti, is an electronic printing calculator

▼ Olivetti's Mercator 20 cash register was designed by Mario Bellini and Perry King in 1981.

■ Roberto Lucci's 1984 Pulsar BE40 electronic scale is manufactured by Zenith.

▼ The Olivetti ETV 300 word processor was designed in 1983 by Mario Bellini.

■ The Olivetti Praxis 35, designed by Mario Bellini in 1980–81, was the first portable electronic typewriter.

■ The LH420 Snow Cat was designed in 1984–84 by Bruno Giardino.

■ This 1984 Bruno Giardino design is an instrument used to measure the hardness of metals. Manufacturer: Officine Galileo.

▼ Designed in 1947 by Giò Ponti, the La Pavoni 47 is an espresso maker for use in restaurants.

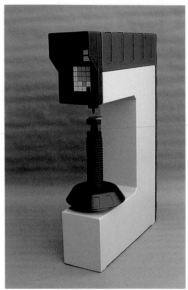

■ The A220 generator, made of die-cast aluminum alloy, cast-iron and high-density polyethylene, was designed for Acme Motori in 1982 by Enrico Picciani.

▼ King Miranda Associates designed the McCullogh Professional chain saw in 1981. It is made of aluminum and nylon parts.

■ The Ormic 10 forklift, designed by Principe Crovetto in 1981–82, can be operated by one person.

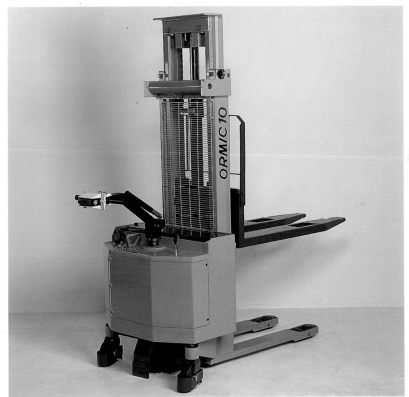

■ The Sigma industrial robot for automatic assembly lines was designed by Rodolfo Bonetto with Naoki Matsugana in 1981–82.

■ The EP2000 automatic labeler,
▼ designed in 1986 by Beppe Benenti, is manufactured by Etipack.

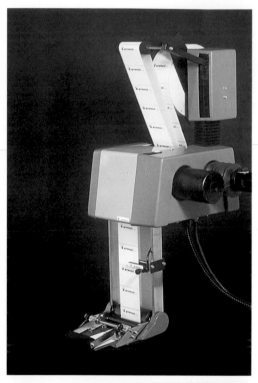

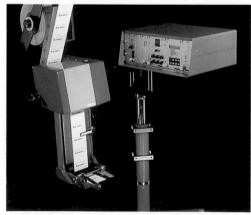

■ The DataLogic TC6,
▼ designed by Beppe
Benenti in 1985–86, is a
solid-state electronic
camera for the direct
reading of computer-read
bar codes and
identification of products
on automatic assembly
lines and conveyor belts.

■ Manufactured by Elkron, the Beppe
Benenti-designed MP 12 is a security system control panel. It was
introduced in 1987.

▼ The DataLogic BS1 photo-electric
cell, designed by Beppe Benenti in
1985, is used as a traffic-control
apparatus in warehouses or on
long-distance conveyor belts.

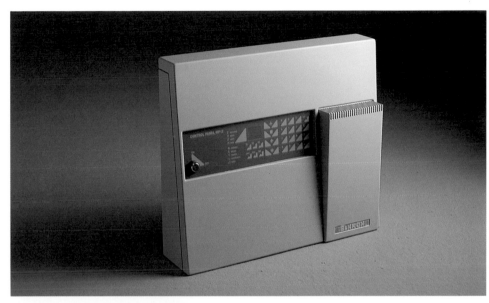

■ Laser instrument for use by dermatologists was designed by Bruno Giardino for Space Laser in 1985.

■ Designed by Beppe Benenti and Walter Olmi in 1980–81, the Eldec miniature decompression computer is used by professional divers at depths of 150-200 meters to allow for safe ascents.

▼ This filter for hemodialysis was designed in 1985 by Giulia Moselli for Sorin Biomedica.

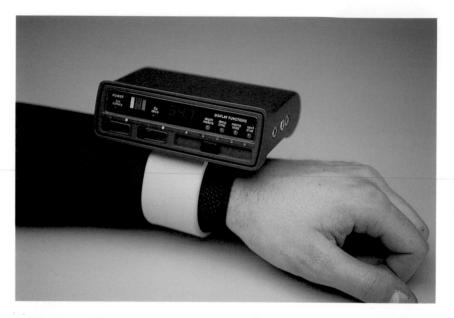

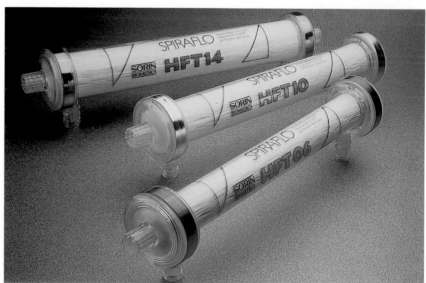

■ The Rotograph 230 from FIAD,
▼ designed by Enrico D'Alto, is an
orthopantograph, used by dentistry
professionals for panoramic mouth
x-rays.

■ Components of the Sorin Biomed-
▼ ica Orion 30 programmable pace-
maker were designed in 1984 by
Jesse Marsh.

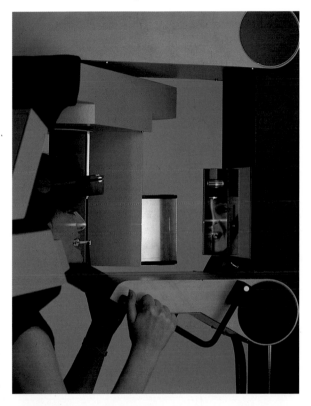

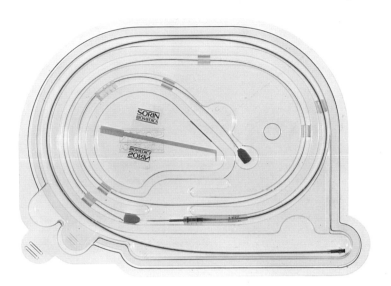

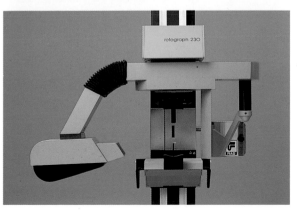

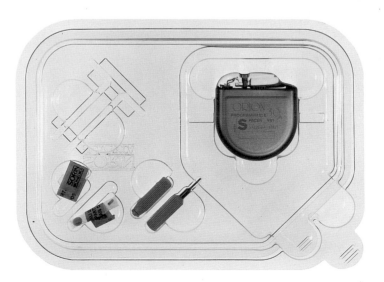

WEAPONRY

■ The A109A TOW helicopter, designed by Agusta from 1975 to 1977, is able to transport eight passengers at a speed of 310 km/h.

▼ The A129 Mangusta helicopter is a multipurpose combat transport, equipped to carry out reconnaissance missions. It was designed in 1987 by Agusta.

■ The A129 Mangusta helicopter offers minimal frontal and lateral target areas.

▼ Designed by Ermanno Bazzocchi from 1980 to 1987, the MB339 is a training aircraft, while the AMX is a tactical-support jet fighter plane. Manufacturer: Aeritalia/Aermacchi.

■ The 92F pistol, by Beretta, is a 9mm parabellum, semi-automatic weapon designed specifically for use by military personnel. Designed in 1975, it was recently adopted as the official sidearm of the United States military. It is also the gun favored by James Bond.

■ The Pm 12S 9mm Parabellum sub-machine gun, designed in 1977, shown with a night-vision scope, is manufactured by Beretta.

▼ The Beretta 81 BB semi-automatic gun, designed in 1983, is marketed for use by the military, civilians and police forces.

■ The 48/AL 12-caliber, automatic hunting rifle, designed in 1946 by Mario Antonio Franchi, was once considered the lightest weight rifle in the world. It weighs 2.8 kgs. Over one million have been sold since its introduction.

▼ The Express SSO bolt-action rifle, designed for hunting use, was introduced in 1985 by Beretta.

▼ A view into the breech of the Express SSO hunting rifle and a closer look at the decorative tooled-metal detailing on the gun.

■ The S.P.A.S. 12/550, an automatic shotgun equipped for use with special low-powered ammunition or for semi-automatic rapid-fire loads, was introduced in 1980 by the Luigi Franchi company.

▼ The S.P.A.S. 12 is designed for use in urban settings or crowded locations.

▼ A 12-caliber, pump-action shotgun, the RS202, was designed by Beretta.

■ The GAQ-4 laser range-finder, introduced in 1986 by Selenia, is used in conjunction with anti-aircraft missile systems.

Sources

The products included in this book are manufactured in Italy and are available to consumers throughout the world. Listed here are the names, addresses, telephone numbers (PH) and telefax numbers (FX) of the Italian manufacturing firms.

Abaco
via Grialba 8
33028 Tolmezzo
PH: 0433/208243013

Abet Laminati
via le Industria 21
12042 Bra
PH: 0172/423611

Acea Manodomestici
28022 Casale Corte Cerro
PH: 0323/60371

Acerbis International
via Brusaporto 31
24068 Seriate
PH: 035/294222

Acme
via Erizzo 43
31049 Valdobbiadene
PH: 0423/73245

Aeritalia
piazzale V. Tecchio 51
80125 Napoli
PH: 081/7252111

Aermacchi
via Sanvito 80
21100 Varese
PH: 0332/254111

Agrati—Garelli
22068 Monticello Brianza
PH: 039/9203414

Agusta
via Caldera 21
20153 Milan
PH: 02/452751
FX: 02/3498729

Alessi
28023 Crusinallo
PH: 0323/6511
FX: 0323/641605

Alfa Romeo
20020 Arese
PH: 02/93392115

Alfatec
via G. Di Vittorio 28
20068 Peschiera Borromeo
PH: 02/5470555
FX: 02/5475059

Alias
via Respighi 2
20122 Milan
PH: 02/5458412
FX: 02/55183133

Alpes Inox
via Monte Pertica 5
36061 Bassano del Grappa
PH: 0424/33400
FX: 0424/36634

Antonelli
60027 Osimo

Arc Linea Arredamenti
via Pasubio 50
36030 Caldogno
PH: 0444/557100
FX: 0444/557922

Arflex
via Monte Rosa 27
20051 Limbiate
PH: 02/9961241

Ariston
viale Aristide Merloni 45
60044 Fabriano
PH: 0732/7011
FX: 02/30702229

Arteluce
via Angelo Faini 2
25073 Bovezzo
PH: 030/2712161

Artemide
via Brughiera
20010 Pregnana Milanese
PH: 02/93291301
FX: 02/93292254

Aurora Due
Strada Abbadia di Stura 200
10156 Torino
PH: 011/2734186

B&B Italia
Strada Provinciale 32
22060 Novedrate
PH: 031/750111
FX: 031/791592

Baglietto
via di Villa Pepoli 23
00153 Rome
PH: 06/5782709
FX: 06/5782709

Bazzani Alberto
via Pusterla 37
20030 Bovisio Masciago
PH: 0362/591001

Beretta
via Pietro Beretta 18
25063 Gardone Val Trompia
PH: 030/837451

Bernini
via Fiume 17
20048 Carate Brianza
PH: 0362/900012
FX: 0362/990429

Bieffeplast
P.O. Box 406
35100 Padova
PH: 049/633466
FX: 049/635323

Bilumen
via Salomome 41
20138 Milan
PH: 02/5064451

Bimarmi
via Prussiano 50/56
PH: 080/921666
FX: 080/921273

Boffi
via G. Oberdan 70
20030 Lentate sul Seveso
PH: 0362/560821
FX: 0362/565077

Brionvega
via Pordenone 8
20132 Milan
PH: 02/2157241

Cagiva-Ducati
via A. Cavalieri Ducati 3
40100 Bologna
PH: 051/405049
FX: 051/406580

Cantieri Riva
24067 Sarnico
PH: 035/910202

Cappellini International
via Cavour 7
22060 Carugo
PH: 031/761717
FX: 031/763333

Carlo Moretti
via Fondamenta Manin 3
30121 Murano
PH: 041/739217

Cassina
via Busnelli 1-P.O. Box 102
20036 Meda
PH: 0362/70581
FX: 0362/76246

Castaldi Illuminazione
via Carlo Goldoni 18
20090 Trezzano sul Naviglio
PH: 02/4454374

Cavazza Design
via Pisacane 10
20129 Milan
PH: 02/719470

Cenedese & Albarelli
Ramo S. Giuseppe 7
30141 Murano
PH: 041/736966
FX: 041/739266

Ceramica Dolomite
32028 Trichiana
PH: 0437/754821
FX: 0437/754383

Cinelli
via Egidio Folli 45
20134 Milan
PH: 02/2158616

Cleto Munari
via Mure Pallamaio 84
36100 Vicenza
PH: 0444/233325

Colle
localitá S. Marziale
53034 Colle Val d'Elsa
PH: 0577/928060

Cottoveneto
vicolo Tentori 12
31030 Carbonera
PH: 0422/396045

Cressi-sub
via M. Mastrangelo 4
16166 Genova Quinto
PH: 010/338003
FX: 010/333741

Dada
Strada Provinciale 31
20010 Mesero
PH: 02/9787337
FX: 02/9789561

Danese
piazza San Fedele 2
20121 Milan
PH: 02/866019
FX: 02/861464

Datalogic
via Candini 2
40012 Lippo di Caldera

De Angelis
via San Nicolao 3
20123 Milan
PH: 02/808881

De Padova
corso Venezia 14
20121 Milan
PH: 02/708413
FX: 02/783201

Delso
via Brescia 15
20063 Cernusco sul Naviglio
PH: 02/9238951

Dolomite
via Feltrina Centro 3
31044 Montebelluna
PH: 0423/20941
FX: 0423/303388

Domopak
corso Buenos Aires 77
Milan
PH: 02/6694551

Driade
S. da Padana Superiore 12
29012 Fossadello di Caorso
PH: 0523/821648

Etipack
via Aquileja 55/61
20092 Cinisello Balsamo
PH: 02/61290621
FX: 02/6174919

Faema
via G. Ventura 15
Milan
PH: 02/2123

Fantini
via Buonarroti 4
28010 Pella
PH: 0322/969127

FAS
via E. Fermi 26
48025 Riolo Terme
PH: 0546/71449

Fatif
via Maniago 12
20134 Milan
PH: 02/2157234
FX: 02/2153151

Ferrari
via le Trento Trieste 31
41100 Modena

FIAD
via Enrico Fermi 38
Trezzano sul Naviglio
PH: 02/4452782

Fiat
corso Marconi 20
10125 Torino
PH: 011/65651

Fila
via Sempione 2/c
20016 Pero
PH: 02/3532241
FX: 02/3538546

Flexform
via Einaudi 23/25
20036 Meda
PH: 0362/74426
FX: 0362/73055

Flos
via Moretto 58
25121 Brescia
PH: 030/280281
FX: 030/290046

Fontana Arte
Alzaia Trieste 49
20094 Corsico
PH: 02/4470051
FX: 02/4476861

Fusital
via Gavazzi 16
20035 Canzo
PH: 031/683392
FX: 0362/924455

Gabbianelli
via S. Pietro all'Orto 11
20121 Milan
PH: 02/791886

Girmi BSR
via Leonardo da Vinci 43
28026 Omegna
PH: 0323/881412
FX: 0323/881956

Gruppo Industriale Busnelli
via Kennedy 34
20020 Misinto
PH: 02/9640221

ICF
via Padana Superiore 280
20090 Vimodrone
PH: 02/2500841

ICM
25066 Lumezzane di Pieve
PH: 030/871691
FX: 030/871450

IDEA
via Camperio 9
20123 Milan
PH: 02/806461

Ideal Standard
via Ampère 102
Milan
PH: 02/28881
FX: 02/2888200

Industrie Guido Malvestio
via Caltana 83
35010 Villanova
PH: 049/5563200
FX: 049/5563502

Interflex
via Indipendenza 161/163
20036 Meda
PH: 0362/76461

Italtel Telematica
piazzale Zavattari 12
20149 Milan

Jacuzzi
S.S. Pontebbaba Km 97,200
33098 Valvasone (PN)
PH: 0434/85141

Jen Elettronica
via Raiale 289
65100 Pescara

Joint
via Pergolesi 15
20124 Milan
PH: 02/6690457
FX: 02/6697809

Kartell
via delle Industrie 1
20082 Noviglio
PH: 02/900121

Kong
via XXV Aprile 4
24030 Monte Marenzo
PH: 0341/641550
FX: 0341/641550

La Pavoni
via Archimede 26
20129 Milan
PH: 02/7496057
FX: 02/7496058

Lamborghini
via le F. Cassani 15
24047 Treviglio
PH: 0363/4211

Lancia
via Vincenzo Lancia 27
10141 Torino
PH: 011/65611

Leitner
via Brennero 34
39049 Vipiteno
PH: 0472/765777

Lorenz
via Marina 3
20121 Milano
PH: 02/5456166
FX: 02/782737

Lualdi Porte
via Brigate di Dio
20010 Mesero
02/9789248
FX: 02/9789463

Luceplan
via Bellinzona 48
20155 Milano
PH: 02/3272240
FX: 02/3272440

Luigi Franchi
via del Serpente 12
25020 Fornaci
PH: 030/341161
FX: 030/347415

Lumina Italia
via Donatori del Sangue
20010 Arluno
PH: 02/9015498

Magis
31045 Motta di Livenza
PH: 0422/768742
FX: 0422/366395

Marcatrè
via Sant'Andrea 3
20020 Misinto
PH: 02/9649451
FX: 02/9649038

Mareno
via Conti Agosti 199
31010 Mareno di Piave
PH: 0438/30222

Mario Sirtori
via Risorgimento 3
22041 Costamasnaga
PH: 031/855128

MAS
via della Chiesa 32
50040 Settimello di Calenzano
PH: 055/8825126

Massarelli
circonvallazione Sud
km.810,200
70045 Bari

Mateb
via Gorizia 8
22100 Como
PH: 031/273181

Mattia & Cecco
via De Amicis 36/g
20092 Cinisello Balsamo
PH: 02/6189453

Maxima
via Trebbia 29
20089 Quinto Stampi
Rozzano
PH: 02/8240151
FX: 02/8259320

Memphis
via Breda 1
20010 Pregnana Milanese
PH: 02/93290663

Meroni
via Diaz 21
20054 Nova Milanese
PH: 0362/43781
FX: 0362/41880

MG Due
via Cesare Battisti 8
20030 Bovisio
PH: 0362/590842

MH Way
via Puecher 1
20090 Fizzonasco di Pieve
Emanuele
PH: 02/90720629

Mobiam
viale Europa Unita 9
33030 Majano
PH: 0432/9521
FX: 0432/952235

Molteni
via Rossini 50
20034 Giussano
PH: 0362/851334
FX: 0362/852337

Nava Milano
via Martin Lutero 5
20126 Milan
PH: 02/2570251
FX: 02/2576205

Necchi
via Rismondo 78
27100 Pavia
PH: 0382/4151

Nikon (Officine Galileo)
via Appiani 12
Milan
PH: 02/6596161

Olivari
via G. Matteotti 140
28021 Borgomanero
PH: 0322/844001
FX: 0322/84684

Olivetti
via Porlezza 16
20123 Milan
PH: 02/8057825
FX: 02/8693924

Oluce
via Conservatorio 22
20122 Milan
PH: 02/782161

Ormic
20060 Masate
PH: 02/95760335
FX: 02/95701091

Parigi Design
50032 Borgo San Lorenzo
PH: 055/8457444

Piaggio
corso Sempione, 43
20145 Milan
PH: 02/3182686

Piaggio
via Cibrario 4
16154 Genova
PH: 010/60041
FX: 010/603378

Poggi
via Campania 5
35100 Padova
PH: 0382/466913

Poliform
via Monte Santo 28
22044 Inverigo
PH: 031/607276

Poltrona Frau
Strada Statale 77 Km 74,5
62029 Tolentino
PH: 0733/971766
FX: 0733/971600

Pomellato
via della Spiga 2
20121 Milan
PH: 02/792812

Quasar
via Bagetti 31
10138 Torino
PH: 011/761572

Quattrifolio
corso Monforte 2
20122 Milan
PH: 02/781498

Rede Guzzini
via le Grazie 31
62019 Recanati
PH: 071/981947

Reer
via Carcano 32
10100 Torino
PH: 011/2054222
FX: 011/859867

Rimadesio
via Tagliabue 91
20033 Desio
PH: 0362/622433

S.I.D.I.
piazza Tricolore 2
20129 Milan
PH: 02/781677

Sabattini
via Don Capiaghi 2
22070 Bregnano
PH: 031/771019

Sambonet
via XXVI Aprile 62
13100 Vercelli
PH: 0161/597219
FX: 0161/597205

Saporiti Italia
via Gallarate 23
21010 Besnate
PH: 0331/274198

Sawaya & Moroni
via Manzoni 11
20121 Milano
PH: 02/8059180

Selenia
via Tiburtina Km. 12.400 2
00131 Rome
PH: 06/43601

Simon International
Superstrada Km 271,500
61030 Calcinelli di Saltara
PH: 0721/895450

Sirrah
via Molino Rosso 8
40026 Imola
PH: 0542/31665

Sisal
via Emilia Pavese 107
29100 Piacenza
PH: 0523/41341

Skipper
via S.Spirito 14
20121 Milano
PH: 02/705691

Snaidero
viale Europa Unita 9
33030 Majano
PH: 0432/959191
FX: 952218

Solari Udine
via Gino Pieri 29
33100 Udine
PH: 0432/4971
FX: 0432/480160

Solzi Luce
via del Sale 46
26100 Cremona
PH: 0372/25712

Sorin Biomedica
13040 Saluggia
PH: 0161/4871

Sottini
via Novara 30
28024 Gozzano
PH: 0322/94666

Stella
via Unità d'Italia 1
28100 Novara
PH: 0321/32251

Stildomus
via Laurentina km 27
00040 Pomezia
PH: 06/9195144

Stilnovo
via Borromini 12
20020 Lainate
PH: 02/9374471
FX: 02/9371074

T & J Vestor
via Roma 117
21010 Golasecca
PH: 0331/964101

Targetti Sankey
via Pratese 164
50145 Firenze
PH: 055/311871
FX: 055/374556

Technisub
piazzale Kennedy 1/d
16129 Genova
PH: 010/530051
FX: 010/541483

Technogym
via G. Perticari 20
47035 Gambettola
PH: 0547/56047
FX: 0547/54046

Tecno
via Bigli 22
20121 Milano
PH: 02/790341

Tessitura Rossini Gaetano
via Roma 9
22041 Costamasnaga
PH: 031/855104

Teuco Guzzini
via Passionisti 40
62019 Recanati
PH: 071/981444
FX: 071/981480

Tre Ti
Strada Statale
n. 87-Contrada
Pescarola
80023 Caivano
PH: 081/8312122

Turri
via G. Parini 7
22060 Parugo
PH: 031/761811
FX: 031/762349

Unifor
via Isonzo
20078 Turate
PH: 02/96350223
FX: 02/96350859

Valli & Colombo
via Concordia 16
20055 Renate
PH: 0362/924621
FX: 0362/924455

Veart
via Moglianese 23
30037 Scorzè
PH: 041/445308
FX: 041/445047

Venini
Fondamenta Vetrai 50
30100 Murano
PH: 041/739955
FX: 041/739369

Vortice
via G. Verdi
20067 Zoate di Tribiano
PH: 02/9064465

Zani
via del Porto 51/53
25088 Toscolano
PH: 0365/641006

Zanotta
via Vittorio Veneto 57
20054 Nova Milanese
PH: 0362/40453

Zanussi
via Cesare Battisti 12
31015 Conegliano
PH: 0438/35741
FX: 0438/362215

Zenith
via Cadolini 34
20137 Milan
PH: 02/5465141

Zeus Noto
via Vigevano 8
20144 Milan
PH: 02/8373287
FX: 02/8370707

Zucchetti
via Molini de Resiga 29
28024 Gozzano
PH: 0322/956121
FX: 0322/956390

Sources/USA

Many of the products included in this book are available to consumers in the United States through the distributors/importers listed here. If the name of the distributor/importer differs from that of the Italian manufacturer, the Italian firm's name is printed in italics below the name of the American firm.

Abet Laminati
725 River Road, Suite 112
Edgewater, NJ 07020
PH: 800/228-2238

Alessi USA
10 Wheeling Avenue
Woburn, MA 01801
PH: 617/932-9444

Alfa Romeo USA
250 Sylvan Avenue
Englewood Cliffs, NJ 07631
PH: 201/871-1234

Arango
Danese
7519 Dadeland Mall
Miami, FL 33156
PH: 305/661-4229

Artemide
Luceplan
1980 New Highway
Farmingdale, NY 11735
PH: 516/694-9292

Atelier International
Acerbis, Arteluce, Cassina, Flos, Marcatrè
30-20 Thomson Avenue
Long Island City, NY 11206
PH: 718/392-0300

Avventura
Carlo Moretti
463 Amsterdam Avenue
New York, NY 10024
PH: 212/769-2510

Becker
Parola
501 Post Road East
Westport, CT 06881
PH: 203/226-8685

Beretta USA
1701 Beretta Drive
Accokeek, MD 20607
PH: 202/364-8020

Cadsana
ICF Italy
East Middle Patent Road
Greenwich, CT 06831
PH: 203/322-5656

Campaniello Imports
Saporiti Italia
225 East 57th Street
New York, NY 10022
PH: 212/371-3700

Casabella
B&B Italia, Sawaya & Moroni
215 East 58th Street
New York, NY 10022
PH: 212/688-2020

Chrysler Italian Imports
Lamborghini
501 Tonnelle Avenue
North Bergen, NJ 07047
PH: 201/865-6262

Crandall-Hicks
Piaggio
30 Oak Street
Westboro, MA 01581
PH: 508/898-2808

Faema
860 Canal Street
Stamford, CT 06902
PH: 203/323-5040

Ferrari North America
777 Terrace Avenue
Hasbrouck Heights, NJ 07604
PH: 201/393-4081

Fiat USA
Fiat, Iveco, Lancia
375 Park Avenue
New York, NY 10152
PH: 212/355-2600

Fibres South
Sisal Collection
P.O. Box 189
Trussville, AL 35173
PH: 205/655-8817

Flos USA
200 McKay Road
Huntington Station, NY 11746
PH: 516/549-2745

Furniture of the 20th Century
Driade, Zanotta
227 West 17th Street
New York, NY 10010
PH: 212/929-6023

Gullans International
Bieffeplast
30-30 Thomson Avenue
Long Island City, NY 11206
PH: 718/937-2310

Hastings Tile
Cottoveneto, Gabbianelli
230 Park Avenue South
New York, NY 10003
PH: 212/674-9700

Interna Designs
Busnelli, Cappellini, Driade, Fontana Arte, Zanotta
6-168 Merchandise Mart
Chicago, IL 60654
PH: 800/468-3762

ICF
Alias, Boffi, Zanotta
305 East 63rd Street
New York, NY 10021
PH: 212/750-0900

IPI
Arc Linea, Sirrah
30-20 Thomson Avenue
Long Island City, NY 11101
PH: 718/482-7440

Kartell USA
P.O. Box 1000
Easley, SC 29641
PH: 803/271-6932

Lighting Associates
Bilumen, Fontana Arte, Lumina, Oluce, Quattrifolio, Stilnovo, Veart
305 East 63rd Street
New York, NY 10021
PH: 212/751-0575

Modern Living
Driade, Zanotta
8125 Melrose Avenue
Los Angeles, CA 90046
PH: 213/655-3898

Nava USA
1771 Post Road East
Westport, CT 06880
PH: 203/454-2037

Olivetti USA
765 U.S. Highway 202
Somerville, NJ 08876
PH: 201/526-8200

Poltrona Frau USA
14 East 60th Street
New York, NY 10022
PH: 212/308-3553

Poltronova International
30-20 Thomson Avenue
Long Island City, NY 11101
PH: 718/482-7660

Riedal Crystal
Venini
24 Aero Road
Bohemia, NY 11716
PH: 516/567-7575

SEE Limited
Driade, Flexform, Zanotta, Zeus/Noto
118 Spring Street
New York, NY 10012
PH: 212/226-0038

Trans Ceramica
Bimarmi
P.O. Box 795
Elk Grove Village, IL 60009
PH: 312/350-1555

Unifor
240 Peachtree Street N.W.
Atlanta, GA 30303
PH: 404/523-2895

Valli & Colombo USA
P.O. Box 245
Duarte, CA 91010
PH: 818/359-2569

Index